GOLDEN ARCHES

GOLDEN ARCHES

*Rising The Ray
Kroc Story*

ALINA HAZEL

ROSE PUBLISHING

CONTENTS

Table of Content

Chapter 5: Trials and Triumphs
5.1 The ups and downs of McDonald's journey through the 1960s
5.2 Kroc's leadership style and management challenges
5.3 Key moments that tested the resilience of the franchise

Chapter 6: Beyond Burgers and Fries
6.1 Diversification and the introduction of new menu items
6.2 Innovations in service, including the drive-thru concept
6.3 McDonald's role in shaping consumer expectations and trends

Chapter 7: Global Expansion
7.1 McDonald's expansion into international markets
7.2 Cultural challenges and adaptations
7.3 The emergence of McDonald's as a global brand

Chapter 8: Legacy and Impact
8.1 Kroc's philanthropy and contributions to society
8.2 The lasting impact of McDonald's on the fast-food industry and American culture
8.3 Reflections on Kroc's legacy and the continued growth of McDonald's

Chapter 9: Challenges and Controversies
9.1 Examination of controversies and criticisms faced by McDonald's
9.2 Challenges in the changing landscape of the fast-food industry
9.3 McDonald's response and adaptations in the face of criticism

Introduction

Brilliant Curves Rising: The Beam Kroc Story

In the archives of business history, there are stories that rise above simple achievement and adventure into the domain of social peculiarities. One such story is that of Beam Kroc and the ascent of the Brilliant Curves. The story unfurls against the background of mid-twentieth century America, where a modest vision transformed into a domain that changed the worldwide inexpensive food industry.

Beam Kroc, an honest milkshake machine sales rep, coincidentally found the amazing chance that would transform him and the culinary scene for eternity. During the 1950s, the cheap food industry was in its beginning stages, with drive-ins and burger joints spotting the American scene. It was against this background that Kroc experienced the McDonald siblings and their imaginative way to deal with inexpensive food.

The story starts with the McDonald siblings, Dick and Macintosh, who had laid out a little yet fruitful burger joint in San Bernardino, California, in 1940. Their framework, known as the Speedee Administration Framework, was a spearheading idea in the food business, underlining proficiency, consistency, and a restricted menu. It was this framework that grabbed the eye of Beam Kroc, an aggressive business person searching for the following enormous thing.

First experience with the McDonald siblings denoted the beginning of an organization that would reshape the American eating experience. The excursion from a solitary California eatery to the notable Brilliant Curves spreading over the globe is a demonstration of Kroc's vision, constancy, and business keenness.

As Kroc dove into the inexpensive food adventure, he confronted various difficulties. Persuading the McDonald siblings to establishment their image was quite difficult. The siblings, at first reluctant, ultimately surrendered to Kroc's influence, conceding him the establishment privileges. This undeniable the introduction of

3

McDonald's Partnership in 1955, with Kroc in charge of an organization ready for exceptional development.

The early years were turbulent, with Kroc hooking to lay out a traction in the serious cheap food scene. Notwithstanding, Kroc's steady quest for greatness and development before long paid off. The presentation of the notable Brilliant Curves, an image now inseparable from inexpensive food, turned into a visual guide for hungry benefactors the country over. The curves weren't just a plan decision; they addressed the doorway to a normalized, effective, and charming feasting experience.

The outcome of McDonald's was not only a consequence of the food served yet additionally the careful frameworks set up by Kroc. The Beam Kroc period acquainted sequential construction system creation with the kitchen, decreasing stand by times and guaranteeing consistency in each burger served. The establishment model permitted McDonald's to grow quickly, transforming it into a commonly recognized name.

Past the business domain, Beam Kroc's effect on American culture couldn't possibly be more significant. McDonald's turned out to be something other than a spot to snatch a speedy dinner; it turned into a social peculiarity, an image of post-war flourishing, and a get-together spot for networks. The coming of the drive-through additional established McDonald's as an image of comfort in the speedy American way of life.

Kroc's story isn't without its intricacies. As McDonald's developed, strains among Kroc and the first McDonald siblings heightened. The siblings at last left the business, offering their stake to Kroc. The progress denoted a defining moment, with Kroc completely assuming control and directing McDonald's towards worldwide strength.

The global development of McDonald's reflected the post-war globalization wave, with the Brilliant Curves turning into an image of American culture around the world. Kroc's capacity to adjust the brand to various business sectors exhibited how he might interpret social subtleties. From Tokyo to Paris, McDonald's risen above its American roots, adjusting menus to suit nearby preferences while keeping up with its center character.

The outcome of McDonald's additionally carried with it analysis and difficulties. The inexpensive food goliath turned into an objective for banters on wellbeing, ecological effect, and the homogenization of worldwide culture. Kroc's heritage is one of both victory and investigation, as Mcdonald's, no matter what, turned into an image of the globalized, speedy current world.

In his later years, Kroc stayed a crucial figure in the business world. His magnanimous undertakings, including the production of the Ronald McDonald House Noble cause, displayed a merciful side to the one who constructed a domain. The magnanimous endeavors pointed toward supporting families confronting clinical emergencies added a human touch to the McDonald's heritage.

As we think about the Beam Kroc story and the rising of the Brilliant Curves, it's difficult to separate from the account from the more extensive setting of post-war America and the resulting globalization of culture. Beam Kroc's excursion from a striving milkshake machine sales rep to the modeler of a worldwide inexpensive food domain is a demonstration of the force of vision, assurance, and flexibility.

The McDonald's Enterprise, with its famous curves, Blissful Dinners, and Play-Places, isn't simply a business achievement yet a social standard that has made history. Beam Kroc's story is an update that occasionally, chasing a fantasy, one might co-incidentally find an open door that reshapes businesses and leaves a getting through heritage.

1. **Brief overview of the American fast-food landscape in the 1950s**

   The American cheap food scene during the 1950s was portrayed by an expanding post-war economy, rural extension, and a social shift towards comfort and proficiency. Rising up out of the shadow of The Second Great War, the US encountered a time of financial flourishing, with families embracing an all the more relaxed way of life. This shift significantly affected eating propensities, bringing about the peculiarity of cheap food.

   In the consequence of the conflict, returning GIs and their families looked for a takeoff from the somberness of wartime proportioning. The 1950s saw a flood in commercialization, and this freshly discovered prosperity added to the ascent of feasting out as a famous decision for families. The expansion of cars and the improvement of a broad roadway framework assumed a crucial part, making it more straightforward for families to travel and enjoy the curiosity of side of the road feasting.

   Drive-ins and cafes exemplified the American cheap food experience during the 1950s. Drive-ins, described via carhops conveying food to benefactors in their vehicles, turned into an image of comfort and relaxed feasting. The drive-in idea took special care of the craving for speed and productivity, permitting families to partake in a feast without the custom of conventional semi-formal eateries. Vehicle culture and the sentiment of the open street were consistently incorporated into the American feasting experience, adding to the ascent of drive-ins as friendly center points.

   Coffee shops, with their chrome outsides and neon lights, likewise assumed a huge part in molding the 1950s cheap food scene. These foundations, frequently portrayed by a retro tasteful, offered a menu going from hamburgers and French fries to milkshakes and pies. Cafes filled in as local area meeting spots, cultivating a feeling of commonality and kinship among supporters. The casual and cordial environment of burger joints spoke to a wide segment, making them an indispensable piece of American mainstream society during this time.

   It was against this scenery of drive-ins and burger joints that the seeds of the in-expensive food transformation were planted. The 1950s saw the development of imaginative thoughts and smoothed out processes that established the groundwork for the quick development of the cheap food industry in the ensuing many years. Speed and effectiveness became central, mirroring the cultural shift towards a quicker paced way of life.

In the midst of this scene, the McDonald siblings, Dick and Macintosh, entered the scene with their progressive Speedee Administration Framework. In 1940, they laid out a little yet effective burger joint in San Bernardino, California, presenting a framework that underscored productivity, consistency, and a restricted menu. The McDonald siblings' methodology denoted a takeoff from the customary burger joint insight, smoothing out tasks to convey a quicker and more normalized feasting experience.

The Speedee Administration Framework was a forerunner to the sequential construction system creation model that would later characterize the inexpensive food industry. It included an improved on menu, fast completion times, and an emphasis on quality fixings. This inventive methodology reverberated with supporters looking for a quicker, more unsurprising feasting experience. The outcome of the McDonald siblings' activity grabbed the eye of Beam Kroc, an aggressive business visionary with a foundation in deals.

Beam Kroc's entry into the inexpensive food story was a defining moment that would shape the business' direction. During the 1950s, Kroc, a milkshake machine sales rep, coincidentally found the McDonald siblings' eatery. Captivated by the potential for diversifying the idea, Kroc persuaded the siblings to concede him the establishment freedoms. This obvious the introduction of McDonald's Company in 1955, with Beam Kroc in charge of an endeavor ready for extraordinary development.

The establishment model presented by Kroc was instrumental in McDonald's quick extension. Diversifying permitted business people the nation over to recreate the fruitful McDonald's equation, transforming the brand into a universal presence in American people group. The smoothed out frameworks, from the kitchen to client care, guaranteed a steady involvement with each McDonald's area, supporting quick, dependable, and quality eating.

The 1950s inexpensive food scene, while assorted with drive-ins and coffee shops, was on a very basic level modified by the McDonald's model. The idea of cheap food developed from a local curiosity to a normalized, cross country peculiarity. The ascent of the Brilliant Curves became inseparable from the changing elements of American culture, reflecting a change in eating inclinations as well as a change in the manner organizations moved toward effectiveness, marking, and development.

As McDonald's kept on flourishing, other inexpensive food chains arose, each carrying its own turn to the quickly advancing industry. Burger Ruler, Taco Chime, and Kentucky Seared Chicken (presently KFC) were among the trailblazers that emulated McDonald's example, adding to the broadening of the cheap food scene. The 1950s laid the foundation for a cutthroat market where development, promoting, and brand character assumed significant parts in molding buyer inclinations.

The social and social effect of cheap food during the 1950s was significant. It turned into an image of innovation, offering a takeoff from customary feasting shows. Cheap food embodied the ethos of a general public embracing pace, comfort, and a break from the custom of formal dinners. The drive-ins and burger joints that flourished during the 1950s reflected an adjustment of dietary patterns as well as a change in the manner Americans mingled and experienced relaxation.

2. **Introduction to Ray Kroc and his early ventures**
Beam Kroc: Engineer of the Brilliant Curves
In the archives of enterprising history, certain people stand apart as visionaries who formed ventures as well as made a permanent imprint on worldwide culture. One such light is Beam Kroc, whose name is inseparable from the notorious Brilliant Curves of Mcdonald's. The tale of Beam Kroc is a demonstration of the extraordinary force of tirelessness, development, and a sharp comprehension of the advancing elements of the American business scene.

Brought into the world on October 5, 1902, in Oak Park, Illinois, Beam Albert Kroc experienced childhood in when the US was on the cusp of significant social and financial changes. Raised by Czech and Clean settler guardians, Kroc's initial years were set apart by humble conditions. His initial introduction to the business world was as a paper cup sales rep, a modest starting that would ultimately lead him to the bleeding edge of the inexpensive food upset.

Kroc's excursion into the domain of cheap food started during the 1950s, a period characterized by post-war flourishing, rural extension, and the ascent of American industrialism. The cheap food scene at the time was specked with drive-ins and cafes, taking special care of a general public that was progressively embracing comfort and proficiency. It was against this scenery that Kroc, a moderately aged milkshake machine sales rep, coincidentally found an open door that would modify the direction of his life.

The defining moment came in 1954 when Kroc got a request for eight Multimixers — machines equipped for creating different milkshakes all the while — from a little eatery in San Bernardino, California. This apparently normal deal drove Kroc to the entryways of a little however inventive foundation run by siblings Richard "Dick" and Maurice "Macintosh" McDonald.

The McDonald siblings had laid out a burger joint in 1940, utilizing a progressive idea they called the Speedee Administration Framework. This framework, a forerunner to the cheap food model, underlined proficiency, consistency, and a restricted menu. The McDonald siblings' eatery was not normal for anything Kroc had experienced previously, and he was enthralled by the smoothed out processes and the potential for development.

It wasn't simply the nature of the food that interested Kroc; it was the siblings' way to deal with business. The Speedee Administration Framework changed the demonstration of eating out from a relaxed undertaking to a fast, unsurprising, and pleasant experience. Kroc perceived the potential for this creative model to rise above the limits of a solitary California café and reclassify the manner in which Americans moved toward cheap food.

Kroc's experience with the McDonald siblings touched off a flash inside him — a dream for a cross country organization of drive-through joints working under a normalized framework. Notwithstanding confronting starting obstruction from the McDonald siblings, who were careful about giving up control, Kroc's relentlessness and faith in the capability of their framework won. In 1954, he persuaded the siblings to allow him the establishment privileges, and accordingly, the excursion of McDonald's Organization started.

The year 1955 denoted a crucial second as the first McDonald's establishment opened in Quite a while Plaines, Illinois. Under Kroc's administration, McDonald's developed from a solitary eatery in California to a quickly growing chain with a presence the country over. Kroc's virtuoso lay not just in perceiving the capability of the McDonald siblings' idea yet in his capacity to change it into a versatile and replicable plan of action.

Fundamental to Kroc's methodology was the establishment framework. Not at all like customary plans of action where a solitary substance possessed and worked various areas, Kroc's vision was to engage neighborhood business people to claim and deal with their McDonald's eateries. This decentralized methodology considered quick extension, as franchisees were put resources into the outcome of their singular foundations.

Kroc's job reached out past simple business keenness; he turned into the central designer of the McDonald's image. The presentation of the Brilliant Curves in 1953 denoted a visual change that would come to represent a drive-through joint as well as a persevering through social peculiarity. The curves, with their strong, brilliant plan, filled in as a guide for hungry benefactors looking for a recognizable and dependable feasting experience.

The outcome of McDonald's during the 1950s wasn't exclusively inferable from the food served; it was the perfection of Kroc's careful scrupulousness. He executed sequential construction system creation in the kitchen, diminishing stand by times and guaranteeing consistency in each burger served. The accentuation on tidiness, effectiveness, and a normalized menu put McDonald's aside in an industry that was all the while tracking down its balance.

The 1950s were a time of fast development and trial and error for McDonald's under Kroc's stewardship. The establishment model ended up being a unique advantage, empowering McDonald's to dramatically extend its range. Before the decade's over, there were many McDonald's areas across the US, each sticking to the standards of the Speedee Administration Framework.

The achievement, in any case, was not without its difficulties. The connection among Kroc and the McDonald siblings became stressed as the organization developed. Strains heightened, coming full circle in the siblings' exit from the business in 1961. Kroc, courageous, moved forward, completely assuming control over McDonald's and situating himself as the main impetus behind the brand.

The worldwide extension of McDonald's reflected the more extensive patterns of post-war globalization. Kroc perceived the possibility to take the Brilliant Curves past American lines, adjusting the brand to suit various societies while keeping up with its center character. This worldwide development, started during the 1960s, changed McDonald's into an image of American culture all over the planet.

Beam Kroc's excursion from an unassuming milkshake machine sales rep to the brains behind one of the world's most unmistakable brands is a demonstration of his innovative soul. The McDonald's Enterprise, under Kroc's initiative, turned out to be something other than an inexpensive food chain; it turned into a social standard that mirrored the changing elements of society.

As the 1960s drew nearer, Kroc's effect on American culture went past the domain of eating. McDonald's turned into an image of post-war idealism, a symbol of success and progress. The notable engineering, the energetically planned Blissful Feast, and the coming of the drive-through additional dug in McDonald's in the texture of American culture.

In his later years, Kroc kept on forming the McDonald's heritage through magnanimity. The formation of the Ronald McDonald House Noble cause in 1974 exemplified Kroc's obligation to rewarding networks. The cause intended to give a usual hangout spot for families with youngsters going through clinical treatment — a demonstration of the sympathetic side of the man behind the Brilliant Curves.

3. **Teaser of the transformative journey ahead**

As Beam Kroc moved McDonald's into the core of American culture, the 1960s proclaimed a period of uncommon development and advancement for the Brilliant Curves. The groundbreaking excursion ahead wouldn't just harden McDonald's as a worldwide force to be reckoned with yet would likewise observe the development of cheap food from a neighborhood oddity to a worldwide peculiarity. Kroc, the visionary designer behind the Brilliant Curves, left determined to shape a business domain as well as a persevering through social symbol.

The 1960s unfurled as a crucial ten years, set apart by cultural movements, innovative progressions, and a powerful social scene.

Against this background, McDonald's arisen as a pioneer, reclassifying how individuals feasted as well as how organizations worked and developed a worldwide scale. Kroc's authority during this period was portrayed by development, flexibility, and an unflinching obligation to the rules that supported the McDonald's image.

One of the key components driving McDonald's outcome during the 1960s was its proceeded with accentuation on consistency and normalization. Kroc, impacted by the sequential construction system creation model, looked to guarantee that each McDonald's café, whether in New York or Tokyo, stuck to similar elevated expectations. This obligation to consistency smoothed out tasks as well as cemented McDonald's way of life as a solid and unsurprising eating choice.

The notorious design of McDonald's eateries, highlighting the indisputable Brilliant Curves, became inseparable from the brand's obligation to giving an inviting and unmistakable space for supporters. The visual allure of the Brilliant Curves, ascending against the background of different scenes, conveyed a feeling of commonality that rose above social and topographical limits. The actual engineering turned into a piece of the McDonald's insight, indicating to clients that they were entering a space where the standards of speed, proficiency, and quality won.

As the 1960s unfurled, McDonald's wandered into worldwide business sectors, a move that would reclassify the idea of cheap food on a worldwide scale. The venture into Canada in 1967 denoted McDonald's most memorable attack outside the US. This essential move not just mirrored the developing outcome of the brand yet additionally displayed Kroc's prescience in perceiving the potential for McDonald's to turn into a worldwide power.

The internationalization of McDonald's wasn't without its difficulties. Adjusting the brand to various societies required a sensitive harmony between keeping up with the center personality and integrating neighborhood inclinations. Kroc, in any case, demonstrated adroit at exploring these intricacies. The menu was adjusted to take special care of territorial preferences, consolidating things that resounded with different palates. The presentation of the Filet-O-Fish in transcendently Catholic business sectors during Loaned and the production of the McArabia in the Center East exemplified McDonald's capacity to adjust its contributions to social and strict subtleties.

Kroc's worldwide vision reached out past menu variation. The promoting techniques utilized in various nations mirrored a comprehension of nearby sensibilities. The famous "I'm Lovin' It" jingle, presented in 2003, was a demonstration of the widespread allure of Mcdonald's, yet during the 1960s, the methodology was more nuanced. Notices were custom fitted to resound with the social subtleties of each market, building up the possibility that McDonald's wasn't simply an American product yet a brand that could flawlessly incorporate into different social orders.

While McDonald's extended its worldwide impression, the 1960s likewise saw the presentation of new advancements that would additionally shape the inexpensive food scene. The advancement of the Enormous Macintosh in 1968, with its unmistakable three-section bun, exceptional sauce, lettuce, cheddar, pickles, and onions, exemplified McDonald's obligation to culinary development. The Huge Macintosh wasn't simply a burger; it was a social peculiarity that rose above its culinary parts, turning into an image of extravagance and fulfillment.

Past the menu, McDonald's advancements reached out to the functional side of the business. The presentation of the drive-through during the 1970s, however not yet acknowledged during the 1960s, displayed Kroc's premonition in expecting the requirement for expanded comfort. The drive-through turned into a sign of the McDonald's insight, permitting clients to put orders without leaving the solace of their vehicles. This development lined up with the more extensive social patterns of an inexorably quick moving way of life, supporting McDonald's status as an image of comfort.

The 1960s likewise denoted a time of expanded contest in the cheap food industry. As McDonald's set its situation as an industry chief, different chains looked to imitate its prosperity. Burger Ruler, Taco Ringer, and Wendy's were among the competitors competing for a portion of the developing inexpensive food market. The opposition prodded a rush of development as each brand looked to separate itself and catch the consideration of an insightful shopper base.

Kroc's reaction to the cutthroat scene mirrored his obligation to remaining on the ball. The accentuation on quality control, functional proficiency, and a tireless quest for consumer loyalty stayed at the center of McDonald's system. The outcome of McDonald's during this period wasn't just about serving food rapidly; it was tied in with conveying a reliably charming encounter that put the brand aside in a packed commercial center.

The cultural changes of the 1960s likewise affected McDonald's way to deal with corporate obligation. As the ecological development picked up speed and familiarity with social issues expanded, companies confronted developing examination. Accordingly, McDonald's started to carry out drives pointed toward addressing concerns connected with squander the executives, natural effect, and local area commitment. The development of McDonald's from a cheap food monster to a dependable corporate resident mirrored Kroc's acknowledgment of the requirement for organizations to adjust to changing cultural assumptions.

The last 50% of the 1960s saw Kroc's job as a visionary stretch out past the bounds of Mcdonald's. His life account, "Crushing It Out: The Creation of Mcdonald's," distributed in 1977, gave bits of knowledge into his pioneering venture and the rules that directed him. Kroc's story wasn't simply a business example of overcoming adversity; it was a demonstration of the extraordinary force of determination, versatility, and a sharp comprehension of shopper conduct.

As the 1960s attracted to a nearby, McDonald's had solidly set up a good foundation for itself as a worldwide peculiarity, with large number of areas crossing landmasses. The Brilliant Curves, when an image of American inventiveness, had turned into a global token of inexpensive food. Kroc's administration had moved McDonald's from a solitary eatery in San Bernardino to a social standard that rose above borders and social partitions.

The extraordinary excursion ahead for Mcdonald's, be that as it may, was not without its intricacies. The resulting many years would bring the two victories and difficulties as McDonald's explored the always changing scene of buyer inclinations, mechanical headways, and cultural assumptions. The account of McDonald's during the 1960s set up for a continuous adventure of development, variation, and social impact that would keep on unfurling in the years to come. As the Brilliant Curves rose against different horizons, they represented an inexpensive food chain as well as a getting through heritage formed by the visionary initiative of Beam Kroc.

Chapter 1

The Visionary Encounter

The tale of Mcdonald's, as a worldwide peculiarity and social symbol, is indistinguishable from the visionary experience between Beam Kroc and the McDonald siblings, Dick and Macintosh. This experience, happening during the 1950s, denoted the intermingling of imaginative thoughts, business discernment, and the beginning soul of cheap food. As Beam Kroc, a moderately aged milkshake machine sales rep, entered the little however progressive universe of the McDonald siblings' San Bernardino café, the seeds were planted for a groundbreaking excursion that would rethink the cheap food industry as well as the way individuals all over the planet moved toward feasting.

In the post-war scene of the 1950s, the US encountered a time of financial flourishing and rural extension. The cultural shift towards accommodation and productivity made ready for the ascent of inexpensive food, with drive-ins and coffee shops becoming famous eating decisions. In the midst of this scenery, the McDonald siblings had laid out their little burger joint in 1940, presenting the Speedee Administration Framework — a creative way to deal with cheap food that underscored speed, proficiency, and a restricted menu.

Beam's first experience with this progressive model came in 1954 when he got a request for eight Multimixers from the McDonald siblings' eatery. Charmed by the huge volume of milkshakes being created, Kroc, with a sales rep's interest, dared to San Bernardino to observe the activity firsthand. What he experienced was a café as well as a fastidiously created framework that would redirect his life and the scene of American feasting.

The McDonald siblings' Speedee Administration Framework was a takeoff from the ordinary eating experience of the time. It included a worked on menu, fast times required to circle back, and an emphasis on quality fixings. The sequential construction system creation model, impacted by the standards of modern proficiency, changed the demonstration of requesting and getting a charge out of inexpensive food into a smoothed out and pleasant cycle. The outcome of this framework resounded with

Kroc, igniting a dream for a cross country organization of drive-thru eateries working under a normalized and replicable model.

The visionary experience among Kroc and the McDonald siblings was not without its difficulties. Persuading the siblings to extend their fruitful idea past their single California café was not easy at all. The McDonald siblings, defensive of their creation, were at first reluctant to give Kroc the establishment freedoms. Their carefulness originated from a longing to keep up with command over the quality and consistency of their image.

Nonetheless, Kroc's steadiness and faith in the capability of the McDonald siblings' framework at last won. In 1954, he persuaded them to concede him the establishment freedoms, denoting the introduction of McDonald's Organization. This earth shattering choice set up for an organization that would reclassify the American feasting experience and establish the groundwork for a worldwide inexpensive food domain.

The launch of the first McDonald's establishment in Quite a while Plaines, Illinois, in 1955 was a milestone second. This occasion denoted the start of McDonald's change from a neighborhood example of overcoming adversity to a public peculiarity. The standards of the Speedee Administration Framework, presently under Kroc's direction, were executed in each establishment, guaranteeing a steady and solid eating experience for benefactors the nation over.

The establishment model presented by Kroc was progressive in the business world. Dissimilar to customary models where a solitary element possessed and worked numerous areas, Kroc's vision was to engage nearby business people to claim and deal with their McDonald's cafés. This decentralized methodology worked with fast extension as well as guaranteed that each franchisee was actually put resources into the progress of their singular foundations.

The 1950s, under Kroc's stewardship, turned into a time of fast development and trial and error for Mcdonald's. The Brilliant Curves, presented in 1953, turned into the visual sign of the brand.

The curves were not simply a plan decision; they addressed a passage to a normalized, productive, and charming eating experience. The design turned into a vital piece of the McDonald's personality, an image that would before long ascent against horizons across the globe.

The outcome of McDonald's during the 1950s was not just about serving food rapidly; it was tied in with conveying a reliably charming encounter that put the brand aside in a jam-packed commercial center. The sequential construction system creation model in the kitchen, the accentuation on neatness, and the essential area of establishments close to parkways and rural regions were all parts of Kroc's fastidious way to deal with business. McDonald's wasn't simply a spot to get a fast feast; it was a social standard that mirrored the changing elements of American culture.

As McDonald's kept on flourishing, the connection among Kroc and the McDonald siblings became stressed. The siblings, feeling underestimated by the extension and changes carried out by Kroc, in the long run chose to leave the business in 1961. This obvious a defining moment as Kroc completely assumed control over Mcdonald's, situating himself as the main impetus behind the brand.

The 1960s, 10 years set apart by cultural movements, mechanical progressions, and a unique social scene, unfurled as a time of phenomenal development and development for Mcdonald's. The internationalization of the brand turned into a vital concentration as McDonald's wandered past American lines, changing from a nearby example of overcoming adversity to a worldwide force to be reckoned with.

The primary worldwide McDonald's opened in Canada in 1967, denoting an essential move that displayed Kroc's premonition in perceiving the potential for McDonald's to turn into a worldwide power. The transformation of the brand to various societies and markets required a fragile harmony between keeping up with the center character and integrating neighborhood inclinations. Kroc's capacity to explore these intricacies was instrumental in McDonald's fruitful globalization.

The actual menu turned into a material for transformation, with provincial varieties acquainted with take care of different palates. The Filet-O-Fish, acquainted with take care of transcendently Catholic business sectors during Loaned, and the McArabia in the Center East were instances of McDonald's obligation to adjusting its contributions to social and strict subtleties. Kroc comprehended that accomplishment on the worldwide stage required something beyond repeating the American model; it required a nuanced comprehension of neighborhood sensibilities.

While McDonald's extended its worldwide impression, the 1960s likewise saw the presentation of new advancements that would additionally shape the inexpensive food scene. The improvement of the Large Macintosh in 1968 exemplified McDonald's obligation to culinary advancement. With its unmistakable three-section bun, extraordinary sauce, lettuce, cheddar, pickles, and onions, the Large Macintosh wasn't simply a burger; it was a social peculiarity that rose above its culinary parts.

Advancements reached out to the functional side of the business too. The drive-through, however not yet acknowledged during the 1960s, turned into a sign of the McDonald's insight. This expansion lined up with the more extensive social patterns of an undeniably speedy way of life, supporting McDonald's status as an image of comfort.

The last 50% of the 1960s saw McDonald's face expanded contest in the cheap food industry. As the brand cemented its situation as an industry chief, different chains looked to copy its prosperity. Burger Lord, Taco Chime, and Wendy's were among the competitors competing for a portion of the developing cheap food market. The opposition prodded a rush of development as each brand tried to separate itself and catch the consideration of an insightful shopper base.

Kroc's reaction to the serious scene mirrored his obligation to remaining on the ball. The accentuation on quality control, functional effectiveness, and a tenacious quest for consumer loyalty stayed at the center of McDonald's methodology. The outcome of McDonald's during this period wasn't just about serving food rapidly; it was tied in with conveying a reliably charming encounter that put the brand aside in a jam-packed commercial center.

As the 1960s attracted to a nearby, McDonald's had immovably laid down a good foundation for itself as a worldwide peculiarity, with huge number of areas traversing mainlands. The Brilliant Curves, when an image of American resourcefulness, had turned into a worldwide symbol of inexpensive food. Kroc's initiative had pushed McDonald's from a solitary café in San Bernardino to a social standard that rose above borders and social partitions.

The groundbreaking excursion ahead for Mcdonald's, nonetheless, was not without its intricacies. The ensuing many years would bring the two victories and difficulties as McDonald's explored the always changing scene of purchaser inclinations, mechanical headways, and cultural assumptions. The narrative of McDonald's during the 1960s set up for a continuous adventure of advancement, variation, and social impact that would keep on unfurling in the years to come. As the Brilliant Curves rose against different horizons, they represented a cheap food chain as well as a persevering through heritage molded by the visionary initiative of Beam Kroc.

The visionary experience between Beam Kroc and the McDonald siblings during the 1950s established the groundwork for the worldwide peculiarity that McDonald's would turn into.

Kroc's capacity to perceive the capability of the Speedee Administration Framework, combined with his tirelessness in persuading the McDonald siblings to establishment their idea, put into high gear an extraordinary excursion that reshaped the cheap food industry. The 1960s, set apart by global development, culinary developments, and expanded rivalry, displayed McDonald's as a social symbol that rose above borders. As the Brilliant Curves arrived at new levels against different horizons, they turned into an image of cheap food as well as of American business venture, versatility, and persevering through social impact.

1.1 Ray Kroc's discovery of Richard and Maurice McDonald's small but successful San Bernardino restaurant

The mid-1950s denoted a vital crossroads throughout the entire existence of American business, whenever an opportunity experience between a moderately aged milkshake machine sales rep and the McDonald siblings — Richard "Dick" and Maurice "Macintosh" — in a little however creative eatery in San Bernardino, California, would get under way a groundbreaking excursion that would reclassify cheap food as well as the actual texture of American culture. The narrative of Beam Kroc's disclosure of the McDonald siblings' foundation is a story of luck, vision, and the combination of enterprising spirits.

Beam Albert Kroc, brought into the world on October 5, 1902, in Oak Park, Illinois, entered the business world with humble starting points as a paper cup sales rep. His initial years were set apart by a progression of adventures, from selling Lily-Tulip cups to functioning as a jazz performer. Kroc's enterprising soul and talent for deals in the long run drove him to the universe of foodservice hardware, where he turned into a merchant for Multimixer milkshake machines.

It was this job as a Multimixer sales rep that would carry Kroc to the McDonald siblings' consideration. In 1954, Kroc got a request for eight Multimixers from a little café in San Bernardino. Interested by the volume of machines mentioned, Kroc chose to explore further. Much to his dismay that this standard business request would lead him to the entryways of a café that would redirect his life and the scene of American feasting.

The eatery being referred to was the brainchild of the McDonald siblings, who had at first settled it in 1940. Their endeavor, unassumingly named "McDonald's BBQ," went through a groundbreaking change in 1948 when the siblings chose to patch up their tasks. They shut the café for remodels and returned it with a progressive idea they called the Speedee Administration Framework.

The Speedee Administration Framework was an extreme takeoff from conventional feasting foundations. It included a smoothed out menu, speedy times required to circle back, and an emphasis on effectiveness in both kitchen and administration. The McDonald siblings had basically applied standards of modern effectiveness to the café business, making a sequential construction system creation model that would change the idea of inexpensive food.

As Kroc moved toward the McDonald's eatery in San Bernardino, he was struck by the sight that looked for him. The activity was not normal for anything he had experienced previously. The siblings had dispensed with carhops and limited the menu to only nine things — burgers, fries, and refreshments. The kitchen was a model of proficiency, with each staff part relegated explicit errands in a synchronized dance of food readiness.

What Kroc saw that day was something beyond an eatery; it was a perfectly orchestrated symphony intended for speed, consistency, and consumer loyalty. The effortlessness of the menu, the shortfall of server team, and the mechanical production system way to deal with food readiness had a permanent effect on Kroc. He saw a little as well as effective nearby diner however an outline for a cross country organization of drive-thru eateries.

The McDonald siblings' methodology resounded with Kroc on different levels. As a sales rep of Multimixer machines, he had experienced various cafes and drive-ins, seeing the difficulties they looked in conveying speedy and predictable assistance. The Speedee Administration Framework offered an answer for these difficulties, introducing a model that could be recreated for a terrific scope.

The progressive idea of the McDonald siblings' idea was typified in the Speedee Administration Framework. It included a worked on menu that wiped out superfluous intricacies, zeroing in on a couple of things that could be delivered rapidly without compromising quality. The siblings had basically normalized the creation cycle, presenting a degree of consistency and productivity that was progressive in the eatery business.

Kroc's acknowledgment of the potential held inside the Speedee Administration Framework was a snapshot of revelation. He saw not simply a neighborhood example of overcoming adversity in San Bernardino yet a versatile and replicable model that could change the manner in which Americans ate. The idea wasn't just about speed; it was tied in with conveying a predictable and charming eating experience, testing the predominant thought that cheap food must be inseparable from split the difference in quality.

The McDonald siblings had accidentally found a recipe that tended to the developing necessities of post-war American culture. The nation was encountering a time of financial success, and families were progressively embracing an all the more relaxed way of life. The McDonald's model adjusted flawlessly with this shift, offering a takeoff from the convention of customary semi-formal eateries and giving a fast and charming other option.

As Kroc dove further into the tasks of the San Bernardino café, he perceived the extraordinary capability of the McDonald siblings' vision. The siblings had systematized their methodology into a bunch of rules that went past the kitchen. From the essential area of the eatery close to roadways to the productive utilization of room and the normalized plan, each part of the McDonald's activity was intended for most extreme effectiveness and consumer loyalty.

Kroc's vision for McDonald's stretched out past the limits of a solitary eatery in California. He saw a potential chance to take the Speedee Administration Framework across the country, presenting a normalized and steady eating experience to networks the nation over. Be that as it may, persuading the McDonald siblings to grow their fruitful idea past their single eatery ended up being an impressive test.

The siblings were at first reluctant to embrace diversifying. They were defensive of their creation, careful about weakening the quality and consistency of their image by entrusting it to other people. Their interests were established in a certified craving to keep up with the honesty of the McDonald's insight, a feeling that Kroc would experience as he left determined to convince them in any case.

Notwithstanding beginning opposition, Kroc's assurance and confidence in the capability of the McDonald siblings' framework continued. He perceived that the Speedee Administration Framework was not only a neighborhood example of overcoming adversity; it was an extraordinary idea with the ability to reshape the whole cheap food industry. After a progression of discussions, Kroc persuaded the siblings to give him the establishment freedoms, denoting a significant crossroads throughout the entire existence of Mcdonald's.

In 1954, the first McDonald's establishment opened in Quite a while Plaines, Illinois, under Beam Kroc's authority. This occasion denoted the authority start of McDonald's Enterprise and the extension of the Speedee Administration Framework past the limits of San Bernardino. The rules that had been fastidiously applied to the California café were currently being duplicated in establishments the country over.

The establishment model presented by Kroc was a change in perspective in the cheap food industry. Dissimilar to customary models where a solitary substance possessed and worked numerous areas, Kroc's vision was to engage neighborhood business people to claim and deal with their McDonald's cafés. This decentralized methodology worked with quick development as well as guaranteed that each franchisee was by and by put resources into the outcome of their singular foundations.

The launch of the Des Plaines establishment in 1955 denoted a turning point, however it was only the start of McDonald's extraordinary excursion under Kroc's stewardship. The standards of the Speedee Administration Framework — straightforwardness, speed, consistency, and consumer loyalty — were carried out in each establishment, making a normalized and dependable feasting experience that reverberated with benefactors the country over.

The 1950s, under Kroc's initiative, turned into a time of fast development and trial and error for Mcdonald's. The Brilliant Curves, presented in 1953, turned into the visual sign of the brand.

The curves weren't simply a plan decision; they were an image that would before long ascent against horizons across the globe. The design turned into an indispensable piece of the McDonald's personality, an obvious prompt that indicated to clients that they were entering a space where the standards of speed, proficiency, and quality won.

The progress of McDonald's during the 1950s wasn't just about serving food rapidly; it was tied in with conveying a reliably charming encounter that put the brand aside in a jam-packed commercial center. The sequential construction system creation model in the kitchen, the accentuation on tidiness, and the essential area of establishments close to roadways and rural regions were all parts of Kroc's careful way to deal with business. McDonald's wasn't simply a spot to snatch a speedy feast; it was a social standard that mirrored the changing elements of American culture.

As McDonald's kept on flourishing, the connection among Kroc and the McDonald siblings became stressed. The siblings, feeling underestimated by the extension and changes carried out by Kroc, ultimately chose to leave the business in 1961. This noticeable a defining moment as Kroc completely assumed control over Mcdonald's, situating himself as the main impetus behind the brand.

The visionary experience between Beam Kroc and the McDonald siblings during the 1950s put into high gear a progression of occasions that would reclassify the scene of American eating and lay out McDonald's as a worldwide peculiarity. Kroc's revelation of the San Bernardino eatery was in excess of an opportunity experience; it was the gathering of two enterprising spirits — one with a progressive idea and the other with the vision to scale that idea to remarkable levels.

The narrative of Beam Kroc's disclosure of the McDonald siblings' little yet fruitful San Bernardino eatery is a demonstration of the extraordinary force of visionary reasoning and enterprising collaboration. The standards of the Speedee Administration Framework, classified in an unobtrusive California restaurant, turned into the plan for a worldwide cheap food realm. As the Brilliant Curves rose against different horizons, they represented a cheap food chain as well as a persevering through inheritance formed by the visionary initiative of Beam Kroc.

1.2 Initial impressions and insights that sparked Kroc's interest

The mid-1950s in America was a period of post-war success, rural extension, and the ascent of American commercialization. It was against this setting that Beam Kroc, a moderately aged milkshake machine sales rep, wound up on an excursion that would prompt the change of the cheap food industry.

The seeds of this change were planted when Kroc, in his ability as a wholesaler for Multimixer machines, got a request for eight units from a little eatery in San Bernardino, California. This normal deal would finish in Kroc's disclosure of the McDonald siblings' imaginative foundation, starting a progression of impressions and experiences that touched off his advantage and set up for the production of McDonald's Partnership.

As Kroc moved toward the McDonald siblings' eatery in San Bernardino in 1954, he probably anticipated a commonplace burger joint or drive-in activity, like the endless foundations he played experienced in his part as a Multimixer sales rep. Notwithstanding, what looked for him was a disclosure — the McDonald siblings had spearheaded an idea that would reform the manner in which Americans moved toward cheap food. Their foundation, which had gone through a change from "McDonald's BBQ" to a smoothed out and proficient model, encapsulated the standards of what might later be known as the Speedee Administration Framework.

The initial feeling that struck Kroc was the sheer volume of Multimixer machines that the McDonald siblings' eatery required. Eight machines meant a degree of interest for milkshakes that was uncommon, particularly for a little neighborhood restaurant. This ignited Kroc's interest and incited him to dare to San Bernardino to observe firsthand the thing was occurring at this apparently genuine foundation.

What Kroc experienced at the McDonald siblings' eatery was a disclosure. The Speedee Administration Framework, which they had fastidiously carried out, changed the demonstration of eating out into a fast, unsurprising, and charming experience. The mechanical production system creation model in the kitchen, the worked on menu, and the shortfall of carhops or server team — all were parts of a framework intended for proficiency and speed. It was a takeoff from the regular eating experience of the time, and it made a permanent imprint on Kroc.

One of the experiences that promptly caught Kroc's consideration was the McDonald siblings' emphasis on straightforwardness. The menu at their café was radically pared down to only nine things — burgers, fries, and drinks. This was an intentional decision pointed toward smoothing out tasks and diminishing the intricacy of food planning. The accentuation on a restricted menu was a takeoff from the pattern of broad contributions tracked down in numerous coffee shops and drive-ins at that point.

The sequential construction system creation in the kitchen was one more key knowledge that reverberated with Kroc. The McDonald siblings had applied standards of modern productivity to food readiness, with each staff part relegated explicit undertakings in a synchronized cycle. This diminished sit tight times for clients as well as guaranteed consistency in the nature of food served. It was a takeoff from the turbulent and variable nature of kitchen tasks in numerous other food foundations.

Effectiveness was not restricted to the kitchen; it stretched out to the whole situation. The shortfall of carhops or team of waiters implied that clients put in their requests at the counter and accepted their food rapidly. The McDonald siblings had basically dispensed with the requirement for carhops and limited the job of conventional team of servers, further adding to the productivity of the activity. This knowledge into the smoothed out help model would end up being an essential component of the McDonald's example of overcoming adversity.

The essential area of the McDonald siblings' café likewise assumed a vital part in molding Kroc's impressions. Arranged close to expressways and in a rural region, the café was decisively situated to take special care of the prospering vehicle culture of post-war America. The comfort of drive-in assistance and the vicinity to local locations added to the openness and notoriety of the foundation. Kroc perceived the meaning of this area system in arriving at an expansive and different client base.

The standards of the Speedee Administration Framework went past the kitchen and administration; they stretched out to the general plan and design of the café. Kroc noticed the normalized and proficient utilization of room, with explicit regions assigned for food arrangement, client requesting, and feasting. The format was intended to work with a consistent progression of tasks, guaranteeing that each square foot of room was used for most extreme productivity.

Kroc's underlying feelings of the McDonald siblings' eatery were not just about the proficiency of the activity; they were likewise about the potential for adaptability. What he saw in San Bernardino wasn't simply a fruitful nearby restaurant; it was a plan for a normalized and replicable model that could be developed a terrific scope. The bits of knowledge into the sequential construction system creation, the improved on menu, and the by and large functional effectiveness sowed the seeds of a dream that would before long emerge into the McDonald's establishment model.

The nature of the actual food was one more aspect that added to Kroc's advantage. Notwithstanding the accentuation on speed and proficiency, the McDonald siblings were unfaltering in their obligation to utilizing quality fixings. The emphasis on consistency in food planning implied that each burger, each fry, and each drink met a normalized degree of value. Kroc perceived that keeping up with high food quality was essential for consumer loyalty as well as for the drawn out progress of the brand.

As Kroc retained the complexities of the Speedee Administration Framework and saw its effect on the eatery's prosperity, he understood that he was not simply managing a nearby peculiarity; he was seeing the potential for a cross country organization of drive-through joints working under a normalized framework. The McDonald siblings had unintentionally found a recipe that tended to the changing requirements of post-war American culture — a general public that was progressively embracing comfort and productivity.

The McDonald siblings' framework offered a takeoff from the conventional feasting experience, testing the thought that cheap food must be inseparable from split the difference in quality. Kroc perceived that the standards encapsulated in the Speedee Administration Framework had the ability to reshape the whole cheap food industry. The straightforwardness, speed, consistency, and consumer loyalty that characterized the McDonald siblings' methodology were the very components that would before long turn into the mainstays of the McDonald's image.

Kroc's experiences into the McDonald siblings' inventive methodology were not just about perceiving a fruitful café; they were tied in with imagining a social peculiarity. He saw the potential for a brand that could rise above provincial limits and become a pervasive presence in the existences of Americans. The underlying feelings framed during that visit to San Bernardino sowed the seeds of a dream that would drive Kroc's persistent quest for transforming McDonald's into an easily recognized name.

The visionary experience between Beam Kroc and the McDonald siblings during the 1950s put into high gear a progression of occasions that would reclassify the scene of American feasting and lay out McDonald's as a worldwide peculiarity. Kroc's underlying feelings and experiences, started by the effectiveness of the Speedee Administration Framework, the effortlessness of the menu, and the obligation to quality, established the groundwork for the making of McDonald's Enterprise. As Kroc set out on the excursion to take the McDonald siblings' idea cross country, he conveyed with him a business opportunity as well as a dream for a social symbol that would shape the way individuals all over the planet moved toward inexpensive food.

Beam Kroc's disclosure of the McDonald siblings' little however effective San Bernardino eatery was a significant second that put into high gear the formation of McDonald's Partnership. The underlying feelings and experiences started by the productivity of the Speedee Administration Framework, the straightforwardness of the menu, and the obligation to quality established the groundwork for Kroc's vision of a normalized and replicable model. Much to his dismay that this opportunity experience during the 1950s would prompt the ascent of a worldwide inexpensive food monster and the persevering through tradition of the Brilliant Curves.

1.3 The meeting that set the stage for a transformative partnership

The gathering between Beam Kroc and the McDonald siblings, Richard "Dick" and Maurice "Macintosh," during the 1950s denoted an essential defining moment throughout the entire existence of American business venture. This experience, set against the scenery of a little yet imaginative café in San Bernardino, California, would establish the groundwork for a groundbreaking organization that reshaped the cheap food industry and led to the worldwide peculiarity known as Mcdonald's. The tale of this gathering isn't just about a deal; it's about the combination of visionary reasoning, enterprising soul, and the acknowledgment of an open door that could reclassify the manner in which Americans moved toward eating.

In 1954, Beam Kroc, a moderately aged milkshake machine sales rep, wound up on an excursion that would lead him to the entryways of the McDonald siblings' café. The experience was not planned; rather, it unfurled naturally because of a standard deal. Kroc, in his ability as a merchant for Multimixer machines, got a request for eight units from the McDonald siblings' foundation in San Bernardino. Charmed by the critical interest for milkshake machines from this apparently little neighborhood café, Kroc chose to research further.

As Kroc moved toward the McDonald siblings' eatery, he probably expected to experience a customary burger joint or drive-in activity. Notwithstanding, what looked for him was a disclosure — a café that exemplified the standards of the Speedee Administration Framework. The sequential construction system creation model, the smoothed out menu, and the accentuation on effectiveness in both kitchen and administration were not normal for anything Kroc had experienced as far as he can tell as a sales rep in the foodservice gear industry.

The actual gathering, happening in the little yet carefully coordinated kitchen of the San Bernardino café, was portrayed by a powerful trade of thoughts, dreams, and shared acknowledgment of potential. The McDonald siblings, defensive of their inventive idea, at first saw Kroc with incredulity. They were careful about entrusting their fruitful framework to an outcast, worried that diversifying could weaken the quality and consistency of their image.

Kroc, then again, was enamored by the inventive methodology of the McDonald siblings. He saw a nearby example of overcoming adversity as well as an outline for a normalized and replicable model that could upset the cheap food industry. The gathering turned into a discussion for the trading of experiences, with Kroc perceiving the groundbreaking force of the Speedee Administration Framework and the McDonald siblings checking the truthfulness and vision of the one who looked to take their idea past the bounds of San Bernardino.

One of the key components that arose out of the gathering was the McDonald siblings' aversion to embrace diversifying. Their defensive position toward their creation was established in a certified longing to keep up with the trustworthiness of the McDonald's insight. In any case, Kroc, driven by a dream that stretched out a long ways past a solitary eatery, looked to convey the extraordinary capability of their idea on a public scale. The gathering turned into a discussion of sorts, with Kroc steadily upholding for the establishment model for the purpose of extending the scope and effect of the Speedee Administration Framework.

Notwithstanding the underlying opposition from the McDonald siblings, Kroc's assurance and influential abilities in the end won. In 1954, he got the establishment freedoms from the McDonald siblings, denoting the introduction of McDonald's Enterprise. The understanding set up for an organization that would reclassify the American feasting experience and lay out McDonald's as a social standard.

The choice to allow Kroc the establishment freedoms was not made gently by the McDonald siblings. They had put long periods of exertion and advancement in fostering the Speedee Administration Framework, and the possibility of entrusting it to an outcast required an act of pure trust. In any case, Kroc's authentic energy, combined with his obligation to keeping up with the quality and consistency of the brand, persuaded the McDonald siblings that he was the ideal individual to take their idea higher than ever.

The establishment model presented by Kroc was a takeoff from the customary plans of action of the time. Instead of purchasing and working various areas, Kroc imagined a framework where neighborhood business visionaries would have the chance to possess and deal with their McDonald's cafés. This decentralized methodology worked with quick development as well as guaranteed that each franchisee was actually put resources into the progress of their singular foundations.

The gathering that brought about the giving of establishment freedoms was not only an exchange; it was the crystallization of a dream that saw the potential for a normalized and replicable model of inexpensive food administration. Kroc, presently furnished with the privileges to establishment Mcdonald's, left determined to take the Speedee Administration Framework from one side of the country to the other. The gathering had laid the preparation for an organization that went past a business game plan — it was a coordinated effort that combined the inventive thoughts of the McDonald siblings with Kroc's innovative intuition and assurance.

The resulting opening of the first McDonald's establishment in Quite a while Plaines, Illinois, in 1955 denoted a memorable second. The standards of the Speedee Administration Framework, presently under Kroc's direction, were carried out in each establishment, guaranteeing a steady and solid feasting experience for supporters the country over. The gathering that prompted the conceding of establishment freedoms had gotten under way a groundbreaking excursion that would reshape the American inexpensive food scene.

As the organization among Kroc and the McDonald siblings set, the elements of their relationship went through changes. The McDonald siblings, feeling to some degree minimized by the development and changes executed by Kroc, ultimately chose to leave the business in 1961. This noticeable a defining moment as Kroc completely assumed control over Mcdonald's, situating himself as the main impetus behind the brand. The gathering that had started the organization among Kroc and the McDonald siblings currently remained as a urgent second in the development of McDonald's into a worldwide force to be reckoned with.

The gathering not just prepared for the development of McDonald's yet in addition featured the job of vision and coordinated effort in the progress of the endeavor.

Kroc's capacity to perceive the extraordinary capability of the Speedee Administration Framework and the McDonald siblings' ability to share their creation with a pariah were essential to the production of McDonald's Company. The gathering, basically, was a juncture of pioneering spirits, a common vision for development, and a pledge to conveying a reliable and charming eating experience.

The establishment model presented by Kroc was progressive in the business world. It permitted nearby business visionaries to turn out to be essential for the McDonald's example of overcoming adversity, cultivating a feeling of pride and local area commitment. The normalized framework guaranteed that whether a benefactor visited a McDonald's in Des Plaines, Illinois, or some other piece of the country, they could anticipate a similar quality, speed, and productivity that had become inseparable from the Brilliant Curves.

The gathering that set up for the groundbreaking organization among Kroc and the McDonald siblings wasn't one minute in time; it was the impetus for a social and culinary unrest. The standards of the Speedee Administration Framework, presently dispersed through the establishment model, reshaped the manner in which Americans moved toward feasting out. McDonald's wasn't simply a cheap food chain; it was a social standard that mirrored the changing elements of American culture in the post-war time.

In the fallout of the gathering, Kroc's vision stretched out past the boundaries of the US. The outcome of McDonald's during the 1950s and 1960s turned into a take off platform for worldwide extension. The gathering that had at first centered around taking the Speedee Administration Framework cross country before long developed into a worldwide undertaking. The ensuing many years would see McDonald's ascent against horizons across the world, turning into an image of American business venture as well as of a globalized cheap food culture.

The gathering that brought Kroc and the McDonald siblings together was a snapshot of good fortune and prescience. It was a convergence of people who, each in their own specific manner, added to the production of a brand that would rise above ages. As the Brilliant Curves rose against different horizons, they turned into an image of inexpensive food as well as of coordinated effort, development, and the persevering through tradition of a groundbreaking organization.

The gathering between Beam Kroc and the McDonald siblings during the 1950s set up for a groundbreaking organization that reshaped the inexpensive food industry. The trading of thoughts, the acknowledgment of potential, and the conceding of establishment privileges denoted the start of McDonald's Organization. The gathering wasn't simply a deal; it was the combination of visionary reasoning and innovative soul that established the groundwork for the Brilliant Curves to rise and turn into a worldwide social symbol.

Chapter 2

Franchising Dreams

The idea of diversifying dreams epitomizes the quintessence of the American enterprising soul, and no place is this more clear than in the tale of Beam Kroc and the introduction of McDonald's Organization. During the 1950s, Kroc, a moderately aged milkshake machine sales rep, left on an excursion that rose above the domain of deals; it turned into a quest for a dream that would reshape the scene of American feasting and lead to a worldwide inexpensive food realm.

Diversifying dreams were not another idea, but rather Kroc's methodology was progressive in its application to the cheap food industry. The gathering with the McDonald siblings in San Bernardino, California, in 1954 denoted the beginning of this vision. The McDonald siblings had made an imaginative and effective framework — the Speedee Administration Framework — and Kroc perceived its potential as a nearby example of overcoming adversity as well as a diagram for a normalized and replicable model that could be diversified on a public scale.

Diversifying dreams is established in the conviction that an effective business idea can be shared and reproduced by others, giving chances to hopeful business visionaries to possess and work their own organizations while profiting from a laid out brand and functional framework. For Kroc, this idea turned into the main thrust behind his tenacious interest to take the McDonald siblings' idea cross country through diversifying.

In 1954, Kroc got the establishment privileges from the McDonald siblings, and the first McDonald's establishment opened in Quite a while Plaines, Illinois, in 1955. This obvious the authority start of McDonald's Organization and the acknowledgment of Kroc's diversifying dreams. The establishment model presented by Kroc was a takeoff from the ordinary plans of action of the time. Rather than purchasing and working numerous areas, Kroc imagined a framework where nearby business visionaries, or franchisees, would have the valuable chance to possess and deal with their McDonald's eateries.

The establishment model offered a pathway for people to accomplish their own innovative dreams. Franchisees could get involved with the laid out McDonald's image, profiting from the achievement and acknowledgment that accompanied the Brilliant Curves. This democratization of business venture, where the fantasy of business possession was open to a more extensive scope of people, turned into a sign of Kroc's vision.

One of the vital components of Kroc's diversifying dreams was the accentuation on neighborhood possession and local area commitment. Not at all like the conventional model where a solitary substance claimed and worked different areas, Kroc's vision was to engage nearby business people who were by and by put resources into the outcome of their singular foundations. This decentralized methodology worked with fast extension as well as made an organization of McDonald's eateries that were well established in their particular networks.

Diversifying dreams were not just about monetary achievement; they were tied in with encouraging a feeling of responsibility and pride among franchisees. Kroc accepted that when people had an individual stake in the progress of their organizations, they would exceed everyone's expectations to guarantee that the quality, administration, and neatness principles of McDonald's were maintained. The progress of each establishment added to the general outcome of the brand, making a harmonious connection between the enterprise and its franchisees.

The diversifying dreams that Kroc sought after weren't without challenges. Persuading the McDonald siblings to embrace diversifying required steady exchange and a showing of Kroc's obligation to safeguarding the trustworthiness of their image. The siblings, at first reluctant to share their creation with an untouchable, ultimately perceived the capability of Kroc's vision and conceded him the establishment privileges. This significant second in the gathering room in San Bernardino set up for the groundbreaking excursion that would unfurl in the next few decades.

The Des Plaines establishment, which opened in 1955, filled in as a model for the McDonald's establishment model. The standards of the Speedee Administration Framework — effortlessness, speed, consistency, and consumer loyalty — were executed in each establishment, making a normalized and dependable eating experience. The progress of the Des Plaines establishment approved Kroc's vision, and soon, more establishments were laid out across the US.

The diversifying dreams stretched out past topographical limits. As McDonald's kept on flourishing in the homegrown market, Kroc put his focus on worldwide extension. The main McDonald's café outside the US opened in Canada in 1967, denoting the start of a worldwide excursion. The diversifying dreams that started in a little kitchen in San Bernardino currently rose above boundaries, societies, and dialects.

Global diversifying brought its own arrangement of difficulties and open doors. Adjusting the McDonald's model to different social settings required a fragile harmony between keeping up with the center standards of the brand and taking care of nearby inclinations. Kroc's immovable obligation to consistency and quality turned into the core values that guaranteed a Major Macintosh tasted a similar whether in Chicago or Tokyo.

The outcome of McDonald's as a worldwide brand can be credited, by and large, to the diversifying dreams that Kroc sought after. The Brilliant Curves rose against horizons across the world, turning into an image of American inexpensive food as well as of a normalized and dependable eating experience. The diversifying model permitted McDonald's to lay out a presence in nations with changing culinary practices, exhibiting the widespread allure of the brand's standards.

Diversifying dreams weren't restricted to Kroc and Mcdonald's; they turned into a worldview for progress in the cheap food industry. Different chains embraced comparative models, perceiving the productivity and adaptability of the diversifying approach. Notwithstanding, McDonald's stayed the leading figure, with its famous curves becoming inseparable from the actual idea of diversifying dreams.

The effect of diversifying dreams stretched out past the corporate level; it contacted the individual franchisees who became business people under the defensive umbrella of the Brilliant Curves. These people, from assorted foundations and different backgrounds, understood their fantasies of business possession through the McDonald's establishment model. The diversifying dreams that Kroc sought after were, basically, a strengthening instrument that permitted people to accomplish monetary freedom and add to their nearby economies.

The examples of overcoming adversity of McDonald's franchisees became tributes to the practicality of Kroc's diversifying dreams. From modest community America to clamoring cities, franchisees became mainstays of their networks. The nearby possession model guaranteed that McDonald's cafés were spots to snatch a speedy feast as well as vital pieces of the neighborhoods they served.

The diversifying dreams that Kroc sought after likewise prodded advancement inside the McDonald's framework. As the brand extended, new menu things were acquainted with take care of different preferences.

Local variations turned into a typical practice, with specific business sectors including things remarkable to their social inclinations. The capacity to offset consistency with adaptability turned into a sign of McDonald's outcome in exploring the intricacies of worldwide diversifying.

The excursion of McDonald's as a diversifying monster was not without its portion of difficulties. Questions between the organization and franchisees, changing customer inclinations, and rivalry from other cheap food chains were obstacles that must be explored. However, the strength of the diversifying model and the getting through allure of the McDonald's image permitted the organization to endure these hardships and arise more grounded.

Diversifying dreams weren't just about growing the quantity of cafés; they were tied in with making a brand that would persevere through ages. As Kroc passed the light to resulting pioneers, the way of life of diversifying dreams persevered. The organization proceeded to adjust and develop, embracing innovative headways, maintainability drives, and changing shopper assumptions while remaining consistent with the center standards of the Speedee Administration Framework.

The tradition of diversifying dreams reaches out to the current day. Mcdonald's, with great many establishments spreading over landmasses, stays a social symbol and an image of the American innovative soul. The diversifying model, when a clever methodology presented by Kroc, has turned into a standard practice in the cheap food industry and then some. The standards of consistency, quality, and neighborhood proprietorship that support McDonald's diversifying dreams keep on being compelling in molding plans of action across different areas.

The persevering through progress of McDonald's is a demonstration of the force of diversifying dreams when combined with a visionary chief. Kroc's capacity to perceive the capability of the McDonald siblings' idea and his commitment to diversifying dreams made a heritage that reaches out a long ways past the inexpensive food industry. The Brilliant Curves, presently an omnipresent presence all over the planet, are an image of an inexpensive food chain as well as of the acknowledgment of innovative dreams for a fantastic scope.

The tale of diversifying dreams with regards to McDonald's is a story of vision, assurance, and the extraordinary force of business venture. Beam Kroc's quest for diversifying dreams was not just about growing a business; it was tied in with democratizing business venture, enabling people to claim and work their own organizations under the pennant of the Brilliant Curves. The diversifying dreams that started in a little kitchen in San Bernardino turned into a worldwide peculiarity, forming the manner in which individuals all over the planet approach cheap food and business proprietorship.

2.1 Kroc's relentless pursuit of franchising the McDonald's concept

Beam Kroc's determined quest for diversifying the McDonald's idea is a story of steadiness, vision, and extraordinary administration that unfurled during the twentieth 100 years. During the 1950s, Kroc, a moderately aged milkshake machine sales rep, coincidentally found the creative Speedee Administration Framework created by the McDonald siblings in San Bernardino, California. What started as a standard deal for Multimixer machines transformed into an excursion that would rethink the American inexpensive food scene and lead to McDonald's Organization.

Kroc's tireless interest can be followed back to his underlying experience with the McDonald siblings and their little yet effective eatery. The standards of the Speedee Administration Framework, which underlined effortlessness, speed, consistency, and consumer loyalty, reverberated profoundly with Kroc. The proficiency and development showed by the McDonald siblings touched off a dream in Kroc — a dream of taking their idea a long ways past the limits of San Bernardino and making it a public, and ultimately, a worldwide peculiarity.

In 1954, Kroc, unflinching by starting obstruction from the McDonald siblings, persuaded them to give him the establishment privileges for their idea. This noticeable the authority start of McDonald's Company and made way for Kroc's persistent quest for diversifying the McDonald's idea. The establishment model presented by Kroc was a takeoff from traditional strategic policies in the cheap food industry. As opposed to buying and working various areas, Kroc imagined a framework where neighborhood business visionaries could claim and deal with their McDonald's cafés.

The launch of the first McDonald's establishment in Quite a while Plaines, Illinois, in 1955, turned into a turning point. It was an acknowledgment of Kroc's vision and a demonstration of the capability of the establishment model. The standards of the Speedee Administration Framework were not bound to a solitary café in San Bernardino yet were presently being duplicated the country over. Kroc's determined interest was filled by a confidence in the extraordinary force of the McDonald's idea — a conviction that the standards of productivity, consistency, and quality could reform the manner in which Americans experienced cheap food.

The steady quest for diversifying the McDonald's idea expected Kroc to explore various difficulties. Persuading the McDonald siblings to embrace the establishment model was only the start. Kroc confronted wariness from investors, potential franchisees, and, surprisingly, inside his own organization. The overall insight at the time scrutinized the reasonability of diversifying in the cheap food industry, and Kroc's whimsical methodology confronted opposition from the people who questioned the supportability of the model.

In any case, Kroc's steady interest was filled by a conviction that went past standard way of thinking. He had confidence in the capability of the Speedee Administration Framework as a nearby example of overcoming adversity as well as a progressive idea that could be scaled on a public and worldwide level. His capacity to pass this vision on to other people, combined with an involved way to deal with critical thinking, empowered him to defeat suspicion and construct an organization of franchisees who shared his enthusiasm for the McDonald's idea.

Kroc's tireless interest was described by an involved and thorough way to deal with each part of the business. From the plan of the eateries to the obtaining of fixings, Kroc looked to keep up with the best expectations of value and consistency. This obligation to greatness turned into a foundation of the McDonald's image and made way for the persevering through outcome of the establishment model.

The outcome of the Des Plaines establishment filled in as evidence of idea for Kroc's tenacious interest. It exhibited that the standards of the Speedee Administration Framework could be repeated, and the McDonald's idea could rise above local limits. Floated by this achievement, Kroc strengthened his endeavors to extend the establishment organization, setting aggressive focuses for the quantity of McDonald's cafés the nation over.

Kroc's determined interest was additionally obvious in his way to deal with choosing franchisees. He looked for people who shared his obligation to the McDonald's idea and were able to stick to the normalized framework. The franchisees weren't simply financial backers; they became ministers of the McDonald's image, liable for maintaining the standards of productivity and consumer loyalty that characterized the Speedee Administration Framework.

As the quantity of McDonald's establishments developed, so did the requirement for an exhaustive and normalized preparing program. Kroc perceived that the outcome of the establishment model relied on guaranteeing that each McDonald's eatery, no matter what its area, stuck to similar standards. The formation of Cheeseburger College in 1961, the very first business preparing focus of its sort, highlighted Kroc's obligation to greatness and the expert advancement of McDonald's franchisees and workers.

The determined quest for diversifying the McDonald's idea wasn't without its portion of difficulties. Struggles under the surface with the McDonald siblings, conflicts with franchisees, and monetary tensions presented obstacles that expected vital route. Kroc's flexibility and steadfast obligation to the McDonald's vision permitted him to defeat these difficulties and steer the organization through times of vulnerability.

Kroc's tenacious interest wasn't bound to the homegrown market. Perceiving the worldwide capability of the McDonald's idea, he left on global extension.

The primary McDonald's café outside the US opened in Canada in 1967, denoting the start of another part in the organization's set of experiences. The persevering quest for diversifying now rose above borders, and the Brilliant Curves started to ascend against horizons across the world.

Worldwide diversifying introduced special difficulties, including adjusting to nearby societies, exploring administrative conditions, and figuring out different customer inclinations. Kroc's active methodology reached out to worldwide business sectors, where he worked intimately with nearby accomplices to guarantee that the McDonald's experience stayed reliable and reverberated with clients universally.

The tireless quest for diversifying the McDonald's idea turned into a worldwide undertaking. The rules that had demonstrated effective in the US were currently applied to assorted markets, each with its own arrangement of difficulties and open doors. Kroc's vision of making McDonald's an omnipresent presence was turning into a reality, and the diversifying model turned into a vehicle for social trade through the widespread language of inexpensive food.

The worldwide outcome of McDonald's wasn't just about trading an American brand; it was tied in with adjusting and coordinating into nearby societies. Kroc's persevering interest required a sensitive harmony between keeping up with the center standards of the McDonald's idea and permitting adaptability to take care of provincial preferences. The presentation of menu things like the Maharaja Macintosh in India and the McArabia in the Center East mirrored the versatility and responsiveness of McDonald's to different business sectors.

Kroc's determined interest wasn't exclusively centered around development and monetary achievement; it likewise stretched out to corporate obligation. McDonald's turned out to be effectively associated with local area drives, supporting nearby causes and associations. The establishment model permitted individual cafés to draw in with their networks, encouraging a feeling of social obligation that became imbued in the McDonald's way of life.

The tireless quest for diversifying the McDonald's idea likewise elaborate advancement in showcasing and promoting. Kroc grasped the force of marking, and the production of the notable Brilliant Curves became inseparable from the McDonald's insight. The presentation of Ronald McDonald as a mascot in 1963 added a lively and engaging component to the brand, particularly interesting to more youthful clients.

Kroc's persistent interest was not without its snapshots of contemplation. As McDonald's kept on developing, the connection among Kroc and the McDonald siblings became stressed. The siblings, feeling to some degree underestimated by the progressions and extensions carried out by Kroc, at last chose to leave the business in 1961. This obvious a defining moment as Kroc completely assumed control over Mcdonald's, situating himself as the main thrust behind the brand.

The persistent quest for diversifying dreams had changed McDonald's from a provincial example of overcoming adversity to a worldwide force to be reckoned with. The standards of proficiency, consistency, and quality that Kroc had advocated were presently implanted in the DNA of Mcdonald's. The establishment model, once addressed by doubters, had turned into a standard practice in the cheap food industry, with McDonald's setting the highest quality level.

Kroc's tireless interest went on into the 1970s and 1980s, set apart by developments like the presentation of the Egg McMuffin and the Blissful Dinner. The idea of diversifying dreams, which started with a solitary café in Des Plaines, Illinois, had turned into a social peculiarity. The Brilliant Curves had turned into a getting through image of American business, and Kroc's heritage as a visionary chief was immovably settled.

Beam Kroc's tireless quest for diversifying the McDonald's idea is a demonstration of the groundbreaking force of visionary initiative and pioneering soul. From the unassuming starting points of a little café in San Bernardino, Kroc's unfaltering obligation to the Speedee Administration Framework and the establishment model reshaped the cheap food industry and made a worldwide social symbol. The tenacious pursuit wasn't just about business extension; it was tied in with democratizing business, cultivating local area commitment, and adjusting to assorted societies. As the Brilliant Curves rose against horizons all over the planet, they represented a cheap food chain as well as the acknowledgment of diversifying dreams on a phenomenal scale.

2.2 Initial challenges and rejections

The excursion of Beam Kroc in his mission to establishment the McDonald's idea was not without its portion of starting difficulties and dismissals. During the 1950s, when Kroc previously experienced the creative Speedee Administration Framework created by the McDonald siblings in San Bernardino, California, much to his dismay that transforming their nearby accomplishment into a public and worldwide peculiarity would be met with distrust and obstruction.

The underlying difficulties started with persuading the McDonald siblings, Richard "Dick" and Maurice "Macintosh," to endow him with the establishment privileges for their idea. At the point when Kroc moved toward the siblings with diversifying, they were at first safe. The McDonald siblings had carefully fostered the Speedee Administration Framework as a reaction to the failures of conventional drive-in eateries, and they were defensive of their creation.

The McDonald siblings' reluctance originated from a certified worry about keeping up with the quality and consistency of their image. They were watchful that diversifying could weaken the special parts of the Speedee Administration Framework and compromise the trustworthiness of their effective equation.

Kroc's underlying endeavors to convince the siblings to embrace the establishment model were met with incredulity, mirroring the test of persuading pioneers to impart their creation to an untouchable.

In any case, Kroc's assurance and conviction in the extraordinary capability of the McDonald's idea drove him to continue. He saw past the quick worries of the McDonald siblings, perceiving that the Speedee Administration Framework had the ability to reform the cheap food industry on a fabulous scale. The underlying dismissal from the McDonald siblings was not a hindrance but instead an impetus for Kroc to refine his pitch and exhibit the worth he could bring to their vision.

The difficulties reached out past the interior elements with the McDonald siblings. Kroc confronted outer incredulity and obstruction, especially while endeavoring to get financing for his aggressive diversifying plans. During the 1950s, the predominant insight in the business world scrutinized the practicality of diversifying in the cheap food industry. The possibility of nearby business visionaries possessing and working their own McDonald's eateries, sticking to a normalized framework, was met with distrust from banks and likely financial backers.

The dismissal from customary monetary establishments constrained Kroc to ponder financing the extension of Mcdonald's. In a showing of his creativity, Kroc went to unpredictable sources, including utilizing his own resources and getting credits from loved ones. This clever methodology mirrored Kroc's obligation to beating deterrents and making his diversifying dreams a reality, even notwithstanding introductory monetary difficulties.

The underlying difficulties and dismissals additionally reached out to potential franchisees. Persuading business visionaries to get involved with an idea that was moderately untested on a public scale ended up being an imposing undertaking. Many had misgivings about the supportability of the establishment model in the cheap food industry, and others questioned the capacity of a normalized framework to flourish outside the setting of a solitary effective eatery in San Bernardino.

Kroc's tenacious endeavors to enroll franchisees involved not just persuading them regarding the productivity of the McDonald's idea yet additionally imparting in them a feeling of enthusiasm and obligation to the normalized framework. The test was to sell an item as well as to sell a dream — a dream of a brand that could rise above geological limits and deal nearby business visionaries a chance for progress under the famous Brilliant Curves.

The dismissal from potential franchisees was, to some degree, an impression of the eccentric idea of Kroc's vision. The cheap food scene of the time was overwhelmed by free and local administrators, and the possibility of a normalized, cross country framework was a takeoff from laid out standards. Kroc's assurance to reshape the business through diversifying required conquering the obstruction of the individuals who had one or two glaring doubts of progress and untested plans of action.

As Kroc kept on confronting difficulties, he drew motivation from the outcome of the first McDonald's establishment in Quite a while Plaines, Illinois, which opened in 1955. The eatery, filling in as a model for the establishment model, showed that the standards of the Speedee Administration Framework could be recreated, and the McDonald's idea could rise above territorial limits. The underlying outcome of the Des Plaines establishment filled in as a substantial model that energized Kroc's determination and given energy to the ensuing development.

One more huge test emerged inside the interior elements of the McDonald's partnership. The McDonald siblings, while at first strong of Kroc's endeavors, found themselves fairly in conflict with where in which he was taking the organization. As Kroc pushed for quick development and changes to the menu, clashes arose between the first vision of the McDonald siblings and Kroc's desires for development.

In 1961, the connection among Kroc and the McDonald siblings arrived at a defining moment, prompting their possible exit from the business. This undeniable a basic crossroads in the McDonald's story as Kroc took command of the organization. The inner difficulties featured the strains between protecting the imaginative soul of the first idea and the requests of scaling the business on a public and worldwide level.

Kroc's capacity to explore these inward difficulties and dismissals required a fragile harmony between respecting the tradition of the McDonald siblings and understanding his vision for McDonald's as a worldwide force to be reckoned with. The takeoff of the McDonald siblings, while a powerful crossroads in the organization's set of experiences, permitted Kroc to completely carry out his diversifying model and drive the brand's development past what was at first imagined.

The underlying difficulties and dismissals that Kroc confronted weren't just hindrances; they were vital to the groundbreaking excursion of Mcdonald's. Every dismissal filled in as a learning an open door, provoking Kroc to refine his methodology, reinforce his pitch, and track down elective arrangements. The creativity and versatility exhibited during these early difficulties became central rules that directed Kroc in his tenacious quest for diversifying the McDonald's idea.

Kroc's capacity to change over difficulties into open doors was likewise clear in his way to deal with development. As the cheap food scene advanced, Kroc perceived the requirement for ceaseless transformation. The presentation of new menu things, for example, the Filet-O-Fish and the Enormous Macintosh, mirrored Kroc's responsiveness to changing customer inclinations and his obligation to keeping the McDonald's menu dynamic and engaging.

The underlying difficulties and dismissals bit by bit changed into wins as McDonald's proceeded with its remarkable development. The Brilliant Curves, once met with suspicion, turned into a getting through image of American business and a social standard all over the planet. The difficulties of persuading the McDonald siblings, getting subsidizing, and enlisting franchisees developed into an outline for progress in the cheap food industry.

The underlying difficulties and dismissals looked by Beam Kroc in his tireless quest for diversifying the McDonald's idea were critical crossroads in the organization's set of experiences. The incredulity of the McDonald siblings, opposition from monetary foundations, and hesitance from potential franchisees were considerable hindrances that expected steadiness, vision, and imaginative critical thinking. Kroc's capacity to defeat these difficulties, gain from dismissals, and adjust to changing conditions established the groundwork for McDonald's change from a nearby example of overcoming adversity to a worldwide social symbol. The tale of McDonald's underlying difficulties and dismissals isn't simply a section in the organization's set of experiences; it's a demonstration of the getting through soul of development and assurance that characterizes the Brilliant Curves.

2.3 The first successful franchise and the model's early evolution

The launch of the first effective McDonald's establishment in Quite a while Plaines, Illinois, in 1955 denoted an extraordinary second in the cheap food industry and laid the basis for the early development of the establishment model. Under the visionary initiative of Beam Kroc, this achievement not just approved the practicality of diversifying the McDonald's idea yet additionally put into high gear a progression of developments and transformations that would shape the fate of the famous Brilliant Curves.

Des Plaines, a suburb of Chicago, filled in as the proving ground for Kroc's aggressive diversifying vision. The standards of the Speedee Administration Framework, stressing effortlessness, speed, consistency, and consumer loyalty, were carefully executed in the Des Plaines establishment. The progress of this debut adventure was not just a demonstration of the allure of the McDonald's idea yet in addition a proof of idea for Kroc's vision of cross country, and ultimately worldwide, extension.

The early development of the establishment model was described by a promise to keeping up with the best expectations of value and consistency across the entirety of McDonald's cafés. Kroc, perceiving the significance of a normalized framework, guaranteed that each establishment stuck to the rules that had made the first McDonald's eatery in San Bernardino a neighborhood achievement. This accentuation on consistency turned into a characterizing component of the McDonald's image and a vital figure its initial achievement.

One of the basic components that added to the progress of the Des Plaines establishment was Kroc's involved way to deal with preparing and functional productivity. Perceiving the requirement for a normalized preparing program, Kroc laid out Burger College in 1961 — the very first business preparing focus of its sort. This foundation turned into the center for teaching franchisees and representatives on the complexities of the McDonald's framework, imparting in them the upsides of proficiency, neatness, and client support.

The early development of the establishment model likewise saw advancements in café plan. Kroc comprehended the significance of making a particular and unmistakable brand picture. The notorious Brilliant Curves, at first brought about by planner Stanley Meston for the McDonald siblings, turned into a focal component of McDonald's marking. The plan of the cafés, with their unmistakable design and the enlightened Brilliant Curves, added to the foundation of McDonald's as a social symbol.

As the outcome of the Des Plaines establishment resounded, Kroc escalated his endeavors to extend the McDonald's organization. The early franchisees were painstakingly chosen people who shared Kroc's obligation to the McDonald's idea and were able to stick to the normalized framework. The development methodology included distinguishing areas with high traffic, guaranteeing perceivability, and adjusting to neighborhood drafting guidelines — a procedure that turned into an outline for future McDonald's areas.

The early development of the establishment model likewise saw the presentation of a public promoting effort. Kroc perceived the force of marking and the requirement for a strong showcasing system to make brand mindfulness. The "Search for the Brilliant Curves" crusade, sent off in the mid 1960s, became inseparable from McDonald's and built up the possibility that a McDonald's eatery could be effortlessly recognized by its famous curves.

Notwithstanding the public promoting effort, Kroc's initial development of the establishment model included territorial cooperatives. These cooperatives pooled assets from franchisees to finance territorial publicizing endeavors. This decentralized methodology took into consideration nearby transformation while keeping a predictable public brand picture. The provincial cooperatives turned into an indispensable piece of McDonald's advertising technique, adding to the organization's capacity to resound with assorted crowds.

The progress of the early establishments and the advancement of the model additionally required developments in production network the board. Guaranteeing a predictable inventory of value fixings was significant for keeping up with the norms of the McDonald's menu. Kroc spearheaded the foundation of a committed provider organization, making a framework where franchisees obtained their unrefined substances from supported providers. This centralization of the production network added to consistency and quality control across the entirety of McDonald's eateries.

The early advancement of the establishment model wasn't without its difficulties. As McDonald's extended, Kroc confronted the sensitive errand of offsetting consistency with provincial variation. The presentation of provincial menu things, taking care of neighborhood tastes and inclinations, turned into a procedure to explore social variety while remaining consistent with the center standards of the McDonald's image. This versatile methodology permitted McDonald's to turn into a worldwide brand while keeping an association with neighborhood networks.

The venture into global business sectors denoted the following stage in the early development of the establishment model. Kroc's vision of making McDonald's a worldwide brand started to emerge as the primary global McDonald's opened in Canada in 1967. The rules that had demonstrated effective in the US were currently applied to different business sectors, each with its own arrangement of difficulties and open doors.

The worldwide extension required a nuanced way to deal with social variation. Kroc perceived the need to fit the McDonald's insight to neighborhood inclinations without compromising the guiding principle of the brand. The early global establishments saw adjustments to the menu to incorporate things that reverberated with local preferences while keeping up with the proficiency and administration guidelines that characterized the McDonald's insight.

The outcome of the early worldwide establishments made ready for additional worldwide extension. McDonald's kept on entering new business sectors, adjusting its menu and tasks to suit the social subtleties of every area. The early development of the establishment model turned into a contextual investigation in globalization, with the Brilliant Curves ascending against horizons across landmasses.

The early outcome of the establishment model additionally provoked developments in café designs. The presentation of the drive-through during the 1970s, a thought at first met with incredulity, turned into a universal element of McDonald's eateries around the world. This advancement mirrored Kroc's obligation to accommodation and openness, taking care of the changing ways of life of purchasers.

The early development of the establishment model wasn't exclusively centered around functional and promoting advancements; it likewise elaborate a guarantee to corporate obligation. As McDonald's kept on developing, the organization turned out to be effectively engaged with local area drives, supporting nearby causes and associations. The decentralized idea of the establishment model permitted individual eateries to draw in with their networks, cultivating a feeling of social obligation that became imbued in the McDonald's way of life.

Regardless of the early achievement and development of the establishment model, challenges persevered. Questions between the organization and franchisees, changing shopper inclinations, and rivalry from other cheap food chains required vital route.

Kroc's strength and unflinching obligation to the McDonald's vision permitted the organization to endure these hardships and arise more grounded.

The early development of the establishment model additionally seen changes in authority. As Kroc ventured down as President in 1977, the organization proceeded to adjust and develop under new administration. The standards of the Speedee Administration Framework, be that as it may, stayed the directing power for McDonald's as it embraced innovative headways, supportability drives, and changing purchaser assumptions.

The kickoff of the first effective McDonald's establishment in Quite a while Plaines, Illinois, in 1955 denoted an essential second in the early development of the establishment model. Under the visionary initiative of Beam Kroc, McDonald's changed from a neighborhood example of overcoming adversity to a worldwide social symbol. The obligation to functional proficiency, consistency, marking, and local area commitment established the groundwork for the persevering through outcome of the Brilliant Curves. The early development of the establishment model turned into a plan for the cheap food industry and a demonstration of the groundbreaking force of diversifying dreams on a worldwide scale.

Chapter 3

Building the Foundation

Building the groundwork of McDonald's Partnership was a multi-layered try that unfurled throughout many years, driven by the vision, assurance, and development of Beam Kroc and the devoted people who added to the organization's prosperity. The establishment building process enveloped different components, from the foundation of the underlying establishment in Des Plaines, Illinois, to the advancement of the organization's functional and promoting procedures, and the venture into global business sectors. This story investigates the central perspectives that formed McDonald's into the worldwide social symbol it is today.

The excursion started vigorously with the launch of the first effective McDonald's establishment in Quite a while Plaines in 1955. This occasion was not simply the introduction of another eatery; it denoted the crystallization of Beam Kroc's vision to establishment the McDonald's idea on a public scale. The standards of the Speedee Administration Framework, underscoring proficiency, consistency, and consumer loyalty, were carefully executed in Des Plaines, setting the norm for all future McDonald's establishments.

The outcome of the Des Plaines establishment filled in as a proof of idea for Kroc's vision. It exhibited that the McDonald's idea, which had flourished in San Bernardino under the stewardship of the McDonald siblings, could be imitated across assorted areas with various franchisees. The fastidious adherence to normalized processes and the accentuation on functional proficiency laid the preparation for the adaptability of the establishment model.

Fundamental to building the groundwork of McDonald's was Kroc's obligation to keeping up with the best expectations of value and consistency across all cafés. Perceiving the meaning of a normalized framework, Kroc laid out Cheeseburger College in 1961. This spearheading adventure was the main business preparing focus of its sort, giving instruction on the complexities of the McDonald's framework, from food planning to client support.

Cheeseburger College turned into a pivotal part in guaranteeing that franchisees and workers across the McDonald's organization were knowledgeable in the standards of the Speedee Administration Framework. The educational plan covered different angles, including kitchen activities, administration effectiveness, and neatness guidelines. This obligation to instruction was meaningful of Kroc's way to deal with building an establishment in light of consistency and greatness.

The early long periods of building the establishment likewise saw developments in café plan. The notable Brilliant Curves, brought about by designer Stanley Meston for the first McDonald's eatery in San Bernardino, turned into a focal component of McDonald's marking. The plan of the eateries, portrayed by the particular engineering and the enlightened Brilliant Curves, added to the foundation of McDonald's as a social symbol. The conscious making of an unmistakable brand picture established the groundwork for McDonald's to turn into an image of American business.

The improvement of a firm and unmistakable brand reached out past actual plan to showcasing procedures. Kroc perceived the force of marking and the requirement for a bound together promoting approach. The "Search for the Brilliant Curves" crusade, sent off in the mid 1960s, became inseparable from McDonald's and built up the possibility that a McDonald's eatery could be handily recognized by its famous curves. This essential promoting drive added to the structure of major areas of strength for a steady brand character.

As McDonald's extended its impression, the organization executed territorial co-operatives to help publicizing endeavors. These cooperatives, contained commitments from franchisees in unambiguous areas, pooled assets to subsidize limited advertising drives. This decentralized methodology considered both public brand consistency and provincial variation, taking care of different crowds while keeping a strong picture.

The establishment building process likewise involved exploring the sensitive harmony among consistency and transformation to provincial preferences. The early advancement of the establishment model saw the presentation of territorial menu things, answering the inclinations of assorted purchaser bases. This versatile methodology permitted McDonald's to turn into a worldwide brand while keeping an association with nearby networks.

The venture into worldwide business sectors denoted a huge stage in building the groundwork of Mcdonald's. The main worldwide McDonald's opened in Canada in 1967, flagging the organization's introduction to worldwide business sectors. The rules that had demonstrated effective in the US were currently applied to assorted global areas, each introducing its own arrangement of difficulties and valuable open doors.

Worldwide development required a nuanced way to deal with social transformation. Kroc perceived the significance of fitting the McDonald's insight to nearby inclinations without compromising the fundamental beliefs of the brand. The early global establishments saw alterations to the menu to incorporate things that reverberated with local preferences while keeping up with the proficiency and administration principles that characterized the McDonald's insight.

One of the critical components in the global extension was Kroc's accentuation on laying out a committed provider organization. The concentrated production network, where franchisees obtained their natural substances from endorsed providers, guaranteed a predictable inventory of value fixings across the entirety of McDonald's cafés. This obligation to quality control and consistency turned into an essential piece of building the establishment for McDonald's worldwide achievement.

The progress of McDonald's was not just ascribed to its functional and promoting techniques yet in addition to its obligation to corporate obligation. As the organization kept on developing, it turned out to be effectively engaged with local area drives, supporting neighborhood causes and associations. The decentralized idea of the establishment model permitted individual cafés to draw in with their networks, encouraging a feeling of social obligation that became imbued in the McDonald's way of life.

In spite of the triumphs, fabricating the groundwork of McDonald's was not without its difficulties. Debates between the partnership and franchisees, changing purchaser inclinations, and rivalry from other inexpensive food chains required key route. Kroc's versatility and enduring obligation to the McDonald's vision permitted the organization to face these hardships and arise more grounded.

The early advancement of the establishment model likewise seen changes in administration. As Kroc ventured down as President in 1977, the organization proceeded to adjust and advance under new administration.

The standards of the Speedee Administration Framework, in any case, stayed the directing power for McDonald's as it embraced mechanical headways, supportability drives, and changing shopper assumptions.

Building the groundwork of McDonald's Partnership was a multi-layered and dynamic cycle that unfurled north of quite a few years. The excursion started with the kickoff of the first fruitful McDonald's establishment in Quite a while Plaines, Illinois, in 1955, under the visionary initiative of Beam Kroc. The obligation to functional productivity, consistency, marking, and local area commitment laid the foundation for McDonald's to turn into a worldwide social symbol. The standards laid out during the establishment building process turned into a plan for progress in the cheap food industry and a demonstration of the groundbreaking force of diversifying dreams on a worldwide scale. Mcdonald's, with its famous Brilliant Curves, remains as an image of cheap food as well as of a visionary way to deal with business that has made history.

3.1 Kroc's role in shaping the McDonald's brand identity

Beam Kroc's job in forming the McDonald's image personality was vital and expansive, stretching out past the foundation of a fruitful establishment model. As the main impetus behind McDonald's Company, Kroc not just changed a nearby example of overcoming adversity into a worldwide social symbol yet additionally ingrained a bunch of standards and values that became inseparable from the brand. This account dives into the diverse parts of Kroc's impact on McDonald's image personality, from functional greatness to promoting developments and corporate culture.

Kroc's visionary authority assumed a focal part in characterizing the functional underpinning of McDonald's and, likewise, its image personality. The standards of the Speedee Administration Framework, accentuating effortlessness, speed, and consumer loyalty, were carefully executed under Kroc's heading. The normalized processes and functional effectiveness became essential to the McDonald's image character, separating the organization in the cutthroat scene of the cheap food industry.

The obligation to functional greatness was additionally set with the foundation of Burger College in 1961. Kroc's prescience in making this spearheading preparing focus showed a commitment to guaranteeing that franchisees and workers were knowledgeable in the complexities of the McDonald's framework. Cheeseburger College turned into a foundation of McDonald's image personality, stressing nonstop preparation and instruction as fundamental parts of keeping up with quality and consistency.

Kroc's impact on McDonald's image personality reached out to the structural plan of the cafés. The famous Brilliant Curves, initially brought about by draftsman Stanley Meston for the McDonald siblings, turned into a focal component of McDonald's marking under Kroc's initiative.

The intentional consolidation of the Brilliant Curves into café configuration added to the production of an unmistakable and conspicuous brand picture. McDonald's eateries, with their novel design and enlightened curves, became inseparable from the brand and hung out in the jam-packed scene of cheap food foundations.

As well as forming the actual character of Mcdonald's, Kroc was instrumental in making the organization's social personality. The obligation to neatness, effectiveness, and client assistance, ingrained through Burger College and functional norms, became characterizing attributes of the McDonald's image. Kroc's accentuation on these qualities imparted a reliable message to clients, supporting that McDonald's was not only a spot to get a speedy dinner yet an encounter established in quality and proficiency.

Kroc's job in molding the McDonald's image character additionally appeared in showcasing and promoting developments. Perceiving the force of marking, he presented the "Search for the Brilliant Curves" crusade in the mid 1960s. This basic yet powerful mission built up the possibility that McDonald's could be handily recognized by its notorious curves, making areas of strength for a relationship with the brand. The accentuation on the Brilliant Curves in showcasing materials and ads added to the foundation of McDonald's as an unmistakable and reliable brand.

The local cooperatives, presented under Kroc's authority, further added to McDonald's image character. These cooperatives, containing commitments from franchisees in unambiguous districts, pooled assets to subsidize restricted advertising drives. This decentralized methodology considered both public brand consistency and provincial variation, encouraging a feeling of local area commitment and fitting the brand to different crowds.

Kroc's impact on McDonald's image character was not bound to the US; it stretched out to the organization's global development. As McDonald's placed worldwide business sectors, Kroc perceived the requirement for social transformation while keeping up with the fundamental beliefs of the brand. The early global establishments saw alterations to the menu to incorporate things that resounded with territorial preferences. This versatile methodology permitted McDonald's to turn into a worldwide brand while holding an association with nearby networks.

The outcome of McDonald's as a worldwide brand was not exclusively credited to its functional and showcasing procedures; Kroc's obligation to corporate obligation assumed a huge part in molding the brand character. As the organization developed, it turned out to be effectively engaged with local area drives, supporting neighborhood causes and associations. The decentralized idea of the establishment model permitted individual eateries to draw in with their networks, encouraging a feeling of social obligation that became imbued in the McDonald's way of life.

Kroc's way to deal with corporate obligation was not only an essential move; it turned into a vital piece of McDonald's image personality. The commitment with neighborhood networks and backing for worthy missions imparted a message of corporate citizenship, adding to the positive view of the brand. McDonald's wasn't simply a cheap food chain; it turned into a mindful corporate substance with a promise to having a constructive outcome on the networks it served.

Notwithstanding the triumphs, Kroc's part in molding McDonald's image character likewise involved exploring difficulties and clashes. Questions with franchisees, changing customer inclinations, and contest from other cheap food chains required key route. Kroc's versatility and unflinching obligation to the McDonald's vision permitted the organization to face these hardships and arise more grounded, adding to the brand's picture of flexibility and versatility.

The mid 1970s denoted a critical change in authority as Kroc ventured down as Chief. Be that as it may, the standards and values he imparted in McDonald's kept on molding the brand personality. The Brilliant Curves, when an image of a diversifying example of overcoming adversity, had turned into a getting through social symbol, addressing a promise to quality, proficiency, and local area commitment.

Kroc's heritage in forming McDonald's image character reached out past his residency as Chief. The organization kept on developing under new administration, embracing innovative headways, manageability drives, and changing buyer assumptions. The primary standards laid out by Kroc, notwithstanding, stayed at the center of McDonald's image character.

Beam Kroc's part in forming the McDonald's image character was great and diverse. His visionary initiative not just changed a neighborhood example of overcoming adversity into a worldwide social symbol yet in addition imparted a bunch of standards and values that characterized the McDonald's image. From functional greatness and promoting advancements to local area commitment and corporate obligation, Kroc's impact pervaded each part of McDonald's character. The Brilliant Curves, under

Kroc's direction, turned out to be in excess of an image; they turned into an encapsulation of a brand that represented quality, proficiency, and a promise to having a constructive outcome in networks all over the planet. Beam Kroc's heritage as a brand engineer isn't simply scratched in that frame of mind of Mcdonald's; it keeps on resounding in each eatery bearing the notorious Brilliant Curves.

3.2 The development of standardized processes and systems

The improvement of normalized cycles and frameworks assumed a vital part in the groundbreaking excursion of McDonald's Organization, laying out it as a worldwide cheap food goliath.

From its modest starting points as a solitary eatery in San Bernardino, California, the organization's obligation to functional effectiveness and consistency turned into a sign of its prosperity. This account investigates the development of McDonald's normalized cycles and frameworks, following their starting points, execution, and getting through influence on the inexpensive food industry.

The underlying foundations of McDonald's normalized cycles can be followed back to the imaginative vision of the McDonald siblings, Richard "Dick" and Maurice "Macintosh." During the 1940s, they looked to address the failures of conventional drive-in eateries by presenting a progressive idea — the Speedee Administration Framework. This framework focused on speed, effortlessness, and a restricted menu to guarantee fast and productive help, making way for the improvement of normalized processes.

The execution of the Speedee Administration Framework at the siblings' unique café in San Bernardino denoted a defining moment. The framework included smoothing out tasks, utilizing mechanical production system procedures, and underlining an elevated degree of accuracy in food readiness. This normalized approach decreased client holding up times as well as guaranteed that each item leaving the kitchen satisfied similar quality guidelines.

Beam Kroc's entrance into the McDonald's story during the 1950s denoted a huge part in the improvement of normalized processes. Perceiving the extraordinary capability of the Speedee Administration Framework, Kroc saw a potential chance to establishment the idea on a public scale. The test, notwithstanding, lay in deciphering the functional proficiency of a solitary fruitful café into a replicable model that could be executed across different areas.

Kroc's job in the improvement of normalized processes included refining and formalizing the frameworks that supported the outcome of the first McDonald's café. He perceived that for the establishment model to succeed, functional consistency was principal. This acknowledgment prompted the making of complete manuals and preparing programs that illustrated normalized strategies for each part of eatery activities, from food arrangement to client support.

One of the vital advancements in the normalization cycle was the foundation of Cheeseburger College in 1961. This imaginative instructional hub turned into the focal point for teaching franchisees and workers on the complexities of the McDonald's framework. The educational program covered everything from kitchen activities and neatness norms to client assistance conventions. Cheeseburger College turned into an image of McDonald's obligation to normalized preparing and assumed a critical part in spreading the standards of functional greatness across the extending establishment organization.

The improvement of normalized processes likewise elaborate a fastidious spotlight on menu disentanglement. Kroc, impacted by the McDonald siblings' accentuation on a restricted and predictable menu, perceived the functional benefits of smoothing out food contributions. The notable McDonald's menu, described by a couple of center things, was intended to guarantee fast help and keep up with consistency in food readiness. This approach recognized McDonald's from rivals and turned into a vital part of its normalized tasks.

The functional normalization was not restricted to food arrangement; it stretched out to café plan and format. The compositional diagram of McDonald's eateries, portrayed by a particular format, kitchen plan, and the notorious Brilliant Curves, added to a steady brand picture. The normalization of eatery configuration assumed a vital part in making a conspicuous and durable brand personality that rose above geological limits.

The execution of normalized processes likewise elaborate a guarantee to quality control and inventory network the board. Kroc perceived the significance of guaranteeing that each McDonald's café gotten reliable and excellent fixings. This prompted the foundation of a committed provider organization, where franchisees obtained their unrefined substances from supported providers. The unified store network added to consistency in item quality across the entirety of McDonald's areas.

The improvement of normalized processes was not without challenges, and Kroc confronted obstruction from doubters who scrutinized the feasibility of reproducing the outcome of a solitary café on a public scale. The overall insight in the cheap food industry at the time leaned toward assortment and customization, and the possibility of a normalized, restricted menu was met with doubt. Kroc's faithful confidence in the groundbreaking force of functional normalization drove him to conquer these difficulties and reclassify industry standards.

The outcome of the first McDonald's establishment in Quite a while Plaines, Illinois, in 1955 denoted an approval of Kroc's vision. The fastidious execution of normalized processes in Des Plaines showed that the standards of the Speedee Administration Framework could be repeated, making ready for additional extension. The progress of the Des Plaines establishment filled in as a substantial illustration of the groundbreaking effect of functional normalization on the cheap food industry.

As McDonald's kept on extending broadly and universally, the normalized processes turned into the bedrock of its prosperity. Each new establishment stuck to similar functional principles, guaranteeing a reliable client experience paying little mind to area. The obligation to normalization permitted McDonald's proportional quickly, turning into a universal presence in urban communities and towns all over the planet.

The getting through effect of McDonald's normalized cycles can be seen in its impact on the more extensive cheap food industry. The progress of the establishment model, described by a normalized menu, functional proficiency, and an emphasis on consistency, set another benchmark for the business. Contenders and novices the same looked to copy the McDonald's model, perceiving the upper hand that normalized processes presented with regards to proficiency, cost-adequacy, and consumer loyalty.

The improvement of normalized processes likewise assumed a critical part in McDonald's showcasing and marking systems. The "Search for the Brilliant Curves" crusade, underscoring the unmistakable visual personality of McDonald's cafés, was moored in the normalization of structural plan. The Brilliant Curves turned into an image of an establishment example of overcoming adversity as well as of a normalized and predictable client experience.

The development of normalized processes went on with McDonald's embracing mechanical progressions. The presentation of the drive-through during the 1970s was a perfect representation of adjusting functional cycles to meet changing shopper inclinations. The drive-through turned into a universal component of McDonald's eateries, offering clients a helpful and proficient method for getting to their number one menu things.

The obligation to normalized processes additionally stretched out to the advancement of new menu things. While the center menu stayed reliable, McDonald's shown a limit with respect to development by presenting items like the Egg McMuffin and the Blissful Dinner. These augmentations exhibited the organization's capacity to adjust while keeping up with the primary standards of functional proficiency and consistency.

The improvement of normalized processes was not safe to analysis, especially in regards to issues of consistency and social variation. A contended that the inflexible adherence to normalized menus and functional methodology gambled homogenizing neighborhood culinary societies. McDonald's answered by integrating territorial menu things, finding some kind of harmony among normalization and customization to take care of assorted customer inclinations.

The improvement of normalized cycles and frameworks remains as a foundation of McDonald's prosperity and an extraordinary power in the cheap food industry. From the spearheading endeavors of the McDonald siblings to Beam Kroc's vision of public and worldwide diversifying, the obligation to functional effectiveness, consistency, and consumer loyalty became imbued in the DNA of Mcdonald's. The foundation of Cheeseburger College, the normalization of menu contributions, the making of a devoted provider organization, and the famous plan of McDonald's eateries generally added to the getting through effect of normalized processes.

The outcome of McDonald's normalized processes reformed the cheap food industry as well as impacted strategic approaches across different areas. McDonald's turned into a worldwide social symbol, with its normalized menu, functional proficiency, and conspicuous brand personality representing the exemplification of inexpensive food achievement. The improvement of normalized processes, established in the standards of the Speedee Administration Framework, is a demonstration of the groundbreaking force of functional greatness and consistency in forming the scene of present day business.

3.3 The challenges of expansion and maintaining quality control

The difficulties of extension and keeping up with quality control have been fundamental to McDonald's development story, exploring a fragile harmony between fast worldwide development and maintaining the brand's obligation to consistency and quality. From its starting points as a solitary eatery in San Bernardino to turning into a worldwide cheap food goliath, McDonald's has wrestled with the intricacies of scaling tasks while guaranteeing that each client experience mirrors the center standards of the brand. This account investigates the complex difficulties that emerged during McDonald's extension and the methodologies utilized to keep up with severe quality control guidelines.

The worldwide development of McDonald's started decisively with Beam Kroc's vision to establishment the effective McDonald's idea. The launch of the first establishment in Quite a while Plaines, Illinois, in 1955 denoted the underlying move toward what might turn into a fast multiplication of Brilliant Curves across the US and at last all over the planet. In any case, this aggressive development plan delivered a bunch of difficulties, boss among them being the need to reproduce the progress of the first McDonald's eatery on a lot bigger scope.

One of the essential difficulties of extension was adjusting the normalized cycles and frameworks to assorted geological, social, and functional settings. The progress of the McDonald's model depended intensely on a painstakingly created arrangement of functional proficiency and consistency, and relocating this model to new areas required a nuanced approach. Each new franchisee must be prepared thoroughly to stick to the normalized techniques illustrated in the manuals and conventions created by Mcdonald's.

Keeping up with quality control despite quick development introduced an impressive test. The gamble of weakening the brand's standing posed a potential threat as McDonald's developed dramatically. Each new eatery needed to convey a similar degree of client experience and stick to the laid out quality guidelines. This challenge turned out to be more articulated as McDonald's extended past the US into global business sectors with different shopper inclinations and culinary societies.

The worldwide extension introduced exceptional difficulties connected with obtaining fixings, adjusting menus, and guaranteeing that the nature of contributions fulfilled McDonald's worldwide guidelines. The organization confronted the fragile errand of offsetting normalized menu with territorial variations took special care of nearby preferences. Presenting provincial menu things turned into a technique to keep up with social responsiveness and importance while maintaining the quality benchmarks set by the brand.

The production network turned into a basic part of McDonald's extension methodology. Guaranteeing a steady inventory of great fixings was basic for keeping up with quality control across the growing organization of eateries. McDonald's laid out a devoted provider organization, smoothing out the obtaining of unrefined components to keep up with consistency in item quality. This incorporated production network the executives considered severe quality control gauges and added to the brand's standing for consistency.

Nonetheless, challenges persevered. Confined store network disturbances, varieties in fixing quality, and contrasts in agrarian practices introduced obstacles that expected cautious administration. McDonald's reaction included laying areas of strength for out with providers, executing quality affirmation measures, and putting resources into innovative work to adjust menu things to provincial limitations while keeping up with the brand's great principles.

The test of keeping up with quality control additionally reached out to the functional side of the business. As McDonald's extended, the organization confronted issues connected with preparing and holding a huge and different labor force. The normalized preparing programs created at Cheeseburger College assumed a urgent part in tending to this test by guaranteeing that each representative, whether in Des Plaines or Tokyo, had a predictable comprehension of McDonald's functional strategies and administration guidelines.

The presentation of new menu things, like the Egg McMuffin and the Cheerful Dinner, added one more layer of intricacy to quality control. While these advancements were intended to take special care of developing shopper inclinations, guaranteeing that they met similar rigid quality benchmarks as the center menu things required fastidious consideration. McDonald's methodology included thorough testing, quality confirmation conventions, and progressing observing to ensure that each new expansion stuck to the brand's quality norms.

Regardless of these endeavors, McDonald's confronted periodic mishaps in quality control. Cases of sanitation concerns and quality-related issues, while moderately intriguing, collected huge public consideration. Every episode represented a danger to the brand's standing and required quick and conclusive activity. McDonald's answered by executing upgraded quality control measures, expanding straightforwardness in its production network, and putting resources into advancements to screen and follow the obtaining of fixings.

The test of keeping up with quality control likewise met with issues of corporate obligation. As McDonald's turned into a worldwide brand, the organization perceived the significance of adjusting its tasks to developing cultural assumptions around well-being, supportability, and moral obtaining. This required changes in accordance with menu contributions, provider rehearses, and corporate arrangements to address concerns connected with sustenance, natural effect, and creature government assistance.

The difficulties of development and keeping up with quality control were not exclusively restricted to functional viewpoints. The social variation expected for worldwide extension reached out to advertising and marking methodologies. McDonald's confronted the undertaking of making promoting messages that reverberated with different crowds while keeping a steady brand picture. The "Search for the Brilliant Curves" crusade, while powerful in the US, expected variations to suit social subtleties in worldwide business sectors.

The test of keeping up with quality control took a mechanical turn as McDonald's embraced developments in computerization and data innovation. The presentation of retail location frameworks, computerized kitchen gear, and advanced requesting stages expected to upgrade functional productivity and further develop request precision. Be that as it may, incorporating these advances while guaranteeing reliable quality guidelines required cautious preparation and execution.

The venture into the computerized domain, including versatile requesting and conveyance administrations, presented new difficulties. Guaranteeing that the nature of food remained positive during the conveyance cycle, adjusting to the inclinations of computerized adroit shoppers, and defending against potential network protection dangers turned into extra elements of the quality control challenge in the cutting edge period.

The difficulties of development and keeping up with quality control were not without intermittent slips up. Mcdonald's, on occasion, confronted analysis for being delayed to adjust to changing buyer inclinations, especially despite contest from quick easygoing and better feasting choices. Answering these difficulties included a sensitive harmony between maintaining the center standards of the brand and embracing developments that resounded with developing buyer patterns.

The excursion of McDonald's additionally saw variances in authority, with changes in chief administration impacting the organization's way to deal with development and quality control. The progress from Beam Kroc's initiative in the last part of the 1970s denoted a change in the hierarchical elements. New initiative brought new points of view, systems, and reactions to the difficulties of a quickly changing industry scene.

The difficulties of development and keeping up with quality control have been characteristic for McDonald's excursion from a solitary café in San Bernardino to a worldwide cheap food force to be reckoned with. The organization's capacity to explore these difficulties mirrors its flexibility, versatility, and obligation to maintaining the standards of functional productivity and quality control. From the beginning of public diversifying to the intricacies of worldwide extension and the advanced age, McDonald's has constantly developed its methodologies to guarantee that each client experience lines up with the brand's commitment of consistency and quality. The continuous moves act as a demonstration of McDonald's obligation to getting the hang of, adjusting, and keeping up with its situation as a famous and persevering through brand in the consistently developing scene of the cheap food industry.

Chapter 4

Shifting Strategies

The development of McDonald's has been set apart by a progression of moving procedures, each answering the unique scene of the inexpensive food industry and changing customer inclinations. From its initial days as a solitary café in San Bernardino to its ongoing status as a worldwide symbol, McDonald's has shown a striking limit with regards to vital variation. This story investigates the critical minutes and all-encompassing patterns that characterize McDonald's moving systems throughout the long term.

The early progress of McDonald's was based on an underpinning of functional proficiency and normalization. Beam Kroc's vision to establishment the McDonald's idea cross country during the 1950s was grounded in the conviction that a normalized framework, underlining rate and consistency, could be duplicated across different areas. This obvious the underlying key shift, changing from a solitary effective café to a versatile establishment model.

The establishment model permitted McDonald's to quickly grow its impression across the US and in the long run around the world. The shift towards diversifying was an essential move for development as well as a reaction to the decentralized idea of the American cheap food industry. McDonald's turned into a pioneer in laying out an organization of franchisees, each working under the normalized framework created by the organization.

As McDonald's extended, the organization confronted the test of offsetting normalization with provincial transformation. The procedure of offering local menu things was an early reaction to this test. Perceiving the assorted culinary inclinations across the US, McDonald's acquainted menu things that cooked with nearby preferences while keeping up with the center standards of functional effectiveness. This provincial transformation turned into a sign of McDonald's procedure, permitting the brand to interface with buyers on a more confined level.

The 1970s saw a huge change in McDonald's methodologies with the presentation of the drive-through idea. This development, at first met with distrust, turned into a unique advantage, lining up with the rising accentuation on comfort in customer ways of life. The drive-through facilitated administration as well as turned into an image of McDonald's obligation to developing with changing buyer ways of behaving. This essential shift mirrored a nuanced comprehension of the market and a readiness to embrace developments that lined up with moving cultural patterns.

The 1980s saw a more articulated center around showcasing and marking as McDonald's looked to harden its situation as a worldwide social symbol. The famous "You Merit a Break Today" crusade and the presentation of Ronald McDonald were key moves to advance the brand as well as to make a close to home association with purchasers. This obvious a shift from the previous accentuation on functional productivity to a more thorough methodology that perceived the significance of brand dedication and shopper insights.

The worldwide development during the 1980s and 1990s was a significant key move for Mcdonald's. The organization wandered into different worldwide business sectors, acquainting the Brilliant Curves with nations with fluctuating social settings. This worldwide extension technique required cautious route of local subtleties, from adjusting menus to obliging social inclinations. McDonald's progress in worldwide business sectors was a demonstration of its functional ability as well as to its capacity to fit systems to fit different worldwide scenes.

The 1990s achieved a change in McDonald's menu procedures with an uplifted spotlight on development. The presentation of better menu choices, like plates of mixed greens and barbecued chicken, was a reaction to the developing customer familiarity with wellbeing and nourishment. This essential shift recognized the need to take special care of changing inclinations and position McDonald's as a brand sensitive to developing cultural worries. The "Made for You" cooking framework, carried out in the last part of the 1990s, was one more essential move to upgrade food quality and customization.

Nonetheless, the 2000s got new difficulties and a shift purchaser impression of cheap food. McDonald's confronted analysis connected with wellbeing concerns, natural effect, and moral obtaining.

Accordingly, the organization carried out a progression of key drives to address these worries. The "Go Dynamic!" grown-up Cheerful Feast, including better choices, and the obligation to practical obtaining of espresso beans were vital moves to adjust McDonald's to changing cultural assumptions.

The presentation of the McCafé idea during the 2000s addressed an essential shift into the espresso and refreshment market. McDonald's perceived the developing purchaser interest for premium espresso choices and looked to profit by this pattern. The McCafé methodology extended McDonald's item contributions as well as situated the brand as an impressive player in the serious espresso industry.

The computerized age achieved another arrangement of difficulties and valuable open doors, provoking McDonald's to move its methodologies to embrace innovative headways. The execution of self-administration stands, portable requesting, and conveyance administrations was an essential reaction to the changing scene of purchaser inclinations and the ascent of online business. These advanced developments upgraded client comfort as well as mirrored McDonald's obligation to remaining at the bleeding edge of innovation.

The 2020s saw a speed increase of advanced methodologies, particularly in light of the worldwide Coronavirus pandemic. The accentuation on drive-through, contactless installment choices, and conveyance administrations became fundamental to McDonald's methodologies to adjust to changing customer ways of behaving. The presentation of the "McDonald's Representing things to come" idea, highlighting modernized feasting regions and improved computerized encounters, exemplified the brand's obligation to remaining in front of developing customer assumptions.

Natural maintainability has turned into a vital focal point of McDonald's methodologies lately. The obligation to maintainable obtaining, lessening waste, and addressing natural worries has been an essential reaction to developing shopper mindfulness and assumptions. McDonald's vow to utilize just enclosure free eggs, feasible fish, and dispense with deforestation from its production network mirrors a more extensive shift towards corporate obligation.

The difficulties presented by the ascent of quick relaxed feasting and changing shopper inclinations for better choices have driven McDonald's to rethink its menu methodologies. The essential presentation of plant-based choices and better decisions mirrors a promise to giving a different menu that takes special care of an expansive range of purchaser tastes. This shift recognizes the requirement for nonstop variation in a quickly changing food scene.

As McDonald's explores the intricacies of a cutthroat market, the organization has progressively embraced straightforwardness as an essential point of support. Conveying healthful data, obtaining practices, and supportability endeavors has become fundamental to McDonald's techniques.

This shift towards straightforwardness mirrors an attention to the significance of building entrust with shoppers and addressing concerns connected with wellbeing, morals, and natural effect.

McDonald's process has been described by a progression of vital movements that answer the developing elements of the cheap food industry and changing buyer assumptions. From the beginning of diversifying to worldwide development, showcasing developments, menu transformations, and embracing computerized advancements, McDonald's has shown a surprising skill to adjust its techniques to remain significant in a unique market. The continuous obligation to natural maintainability, straightforwardness, and menu expansion mirrors McDonald's acknowledgment of the requirement for ceaseless advancement because of cultural movements. As McDonald's keeps on exploring the future, its methodologies will without a doubt be formed by a promise to development, responsiveness, and a commitment to meeting the consistently changing necessities of its different client base.

4.1 Introduction of the iconic Golden Arches and the development of a recognizable brand

The presentation of the notorious Brilliant Curves remains as a crucial part in the improvement of McDonald's into a worldwide social peculiarity. These curves, at first brought about by engineer Stanley Meston for the McDonald siblings' San Bernardino café, developed past simple design components to turn into a strong image of the brand. This story investigates the beginnings of the Brilliant Curves, their joining into the McDonald's image, and their job in making an unmistakable and getting through worldwide character.

In the mid 1950s, as Beam Kroc went into an establishment concurrence with the McDonald siblings, he perceived the potential for McDonald's to rise above its neighborhood achievement. The test was not exclusively to reproduce the functional productivity of the first San Bernardino café yet in addition to make a visual character that could be generally connected with the brand. This undeniable the beginning of the Brilliant Curves.

Stanley Meston, the designer entrusted with planning the new McDonald's areas, conceptualized the notable curves as an unmistakable and eye catching component. The first plan highlighted two huge yellow curves outlining the entry of the café, making an outwardly striking and noteworthy picture. The plan was building style as well as a conscious work to make McDonald's quickly unmistakable in the personalities of clients.

The Brilliant Curves were in excess of a plan decision; they encapsulated the standards of consistency and consistency that were necessary to McDonald's functional model. The purposeful utilization of radiant yellow in the curves was attractive as well as represented warmth and benevolence. The decision of variety was key, making an enticing and congenial vibe that lined up with the brand's obligation to a positive client experience.

As McDonald's left on its excursion of public diversifying, the Brilliant Curves turned into a binding together component across all areas. The curves were not only a plan include; they were an image of a normalized and replicable framework that franchisees could trust. Each new McDonald's café, no matter what its area, integrated the Brilliant Curves into its plan, building up the brand's visual personality.

The essential combination of the Brilliant Curves into the McDonald's image was additionally highlighted by the presentation of the "Search for the Brilliant Curves" advertising effort in the mid 1960s. This mission stressed the curves as an unmistakable and effectively conspicuous image that would direct clients to McDonald's eateries. The straightforwardness of the message passed on the brand's certainty that the Brilliant Curves had become inseparable from the McDonald's insight.

The Brilliant Curves turned into a basic piece of McDonald's more extensive marking techniques. The curves were not only a visual identifier; they addressed a promise to quality, productivity, and a normalized client experience. The curves enhanced everything from signage and bundling to showcasing materials, making a firm and immediately recognizable brand picture. McDonald's cafés, with their enlightened Brilliant Curves, became reference points in the cheap food scene, welcoming clients into a universe of recognizable and reliable contributions.

The curves were not static; they developed throughout the long term because of configuration drifts and changing brand accounts. The progress from the Speedee character, an early mascot for Mcdonald's, to the independent Brilliant Curves mirrored an essential shift. The curves rose above the requirement for a mascot; they turned into the mascot, exemplifying the quintessence of the brand in a straightforward and generally conspicuous structure.

The worldwide extension of McDonald's during the 1970s and 1980s carried the Brilliant Curves to different societies and scenes. The flexibility of the curves to various building styles and conditions built up their general allure. The curves turned into a social symbol, representing a drive-thru eatery as well as a more extensive portrayal of American culture and free enterprise.

The joining of the Brilliant Curves into the worldwide marking of McDonald's required a nuanced approach. While keeping a steady visual character, McDonald's perceived the significance of social responsiveness. In certain nations, the curves were adjusted to mix consistently with neighborhood feel, showing an essential harmony between worldwide marking and nearby pertinence.

The Brilliant Curves likewise assumed a urgent part in McDonald's showcasing systems. The curves were utilized as a visual mental helper, making areas of strength for a between the brand and the particular shape.

The "I'm Lovin' It" crusade, sent off in 2003, built up the profound association with the Brilliant Curves, situating McDonald's as where clients could encounter bliss and fulfillment.

The getting through tradition of the Brilliant Curves lies in their capacity to rise above their utilitarian beginning and become an image profoundly implanted in mainstream society. The curves have been highlighted in craftsmanship, writing, and movies, turning into a shorthand for the idea of cheap food itself. The curves, with their general acknowledgment, have turned into a piece of the worldwide visual language, a demonstration of the progress of McDonald's in making a brand character that rises above borders.

In any case, the excursion of the Brilliant Curves has not been without challenges. Notwithstanding social moves and changing view of inexpensive food, McDonald's has needed to adjust its marking methodologies constantly. The curves, while notorious, have additionally confronted reactions and debates. McDonald's reaction has been vital, consolidating changes in plan, informing, and showcasing to address developing customer assumptions.

As of late, McDonald's has embraced a more contemporary and smoothed out plan approach for its cafés. The Brilliant Curves, while holding their notable structure, have been introduced in a more current and moderate design. This essential shift lines up with more extensive patterns in plan and marking, mirroring a promise to remaining important in a dynamic and serious market.

The Brilliant Curves, when an image of a neighborhood example of overcoming adversity, have turned into a worldwide social symbol. Their excursion from a structural component in a little California town to a generally perceived image of cheap food reflects the development of McDonald's itself. The curves are not only a logo; they address a bunch of values and a guarantee to clients — a commitment of consistency, quality, and a natural encounter, regardless of where on earth one experiences them.

The presentation of the famous Brilliant Curves denoted an essential defining moment in McDonald's set of experiences. What started as a commonsense structural plan decision developed into a strong image that rose above its utilitarian beginnings. The Brilliant Curves turned into the substance of Mcdonald's, typifying the standards of consistency and quality that characterize the brand. From the beginning of diversifying to the difficulties of worldwide development, the Brilliant Curves have remained as a visual anchor in the consistently advancing story of Mcdonald's, an image that keeps on bringing out a feeling of commonality and acknowledgment in the hearts and brains of buyers all over the planet.

4.2 Marketing and advertising innovations that propelled McDonald's into popular culture

The excursion of McDonald's into mainstream society has been firmly entwined with its creative promoting and publicizing systems. From its initial days as a neighborhood inexpensive food example of overcoming adversity to its ongoing status as a worldwide social symbol, McDonald's has utilized innovativeness, consistency, and versatility to catch the creative mind of buyers. This story investigates the vital showcasing and publicizing developments that impelled McDonald's into mainstream society, forming its personality and laying out it as a universal presence in the worldwide customer scene.

During the 1950s, as McDonald's started its public diversifying under the initiative of Beam Kroc, the organization perceived the significance of making a strong and conspicuous brand picture. The notorious Brilliant Curves, presented by draftsman Stanley Meston, turned into a focal component of McDonald's visual character. This engineering highlight was unmistakable as well as loaned itself flawlessly to promoting and publicizing.

The principal significant promoting development that put McDonald's aside was the presentation of the "Speedee Administration Framework," which accentuated the speed and effectiveness of the eatery's tasks. This framework established the groundwork for McDonald's promoting by featuring a vital part of the brand — speedy and helpful help. Showcasing messages started to underscore the idea of "inexpensive food," and the Speedee character, an early mascot, represented the brand's obligation to rapid help.

The 1960s saw a critical showcasing shift with the presentation of the famous "Search for the Brilliant Curves" crusade. This undeniable a takeoff from conventional promoting approaches, as McDonald's centered around making a visual image that could rise above language boundaries and be generally perceived. The mission urged clients to connect the Brilliant Curves with a dependable and recognizable feasting experience, cultivating a feeling of confidence in the brand.

One more earth shattering showcasing advancement during the 1960s was the recruiting of the principal promoting organization committed solely to McDonald's — Leo Burnett. This organization prompted the production of the persevering through motto "I'm Lovin' It," which appeared in 2003. Be that as it may, Leo Burnett's effect on McDonald's advertising started before with the presentation of important characters like Ronald McDonald, Frown, and the Hamburglar. These characters added a lively and engaging aspect to McDonald's promoting, adding to the brand's capacity to interface with a wide crowd, particularly youngsters.

The 1970s saw the send off of the "You Merit a Break Today" crusade, which reverberated with buyers by introducing McDonald's as where people could have some time off from their chaotic resides and partake in a helpful and fulfilling dinner. This mission denoted an essential move towards partner the brand with close to home prosperity and unwinding, making a positive and optimistic picture that stretched out past the utilitarian parts of cheap food.

The 1980s saw McDonald's growing its showcasing arrive at through essential organizations and sponsorships. The joint effort with Disney for the production of the McDonald's Blissful Dinner, highlighting well known Disney characters, was a masterstroke in promoting to youngsters and families. The Blissful Dinner turned into a mark item as well as hardened McDonald's as a family-accommodating brand. The cooperative energy among McDonald's and Disney reached out to limited time connections with blockbuster films, further implanting the brand in mainstream society.

The 1990s denoted a shift towards more comprehensive and various showcasing systems. McDonald's ads progressively highlighted a cross-segment of society, reflecting various ages, nationalities, and foundations. This inclusivity reflected changing cultural standards as well as situated McDonald's as a brand for everybody. The promoting messages zeroed in on making a feeling of local area and shared encounters around the eating table at Mcdonald's.

The turn of the thousand years achieved one of the main promoting efforts in McDonald's set of experiences — the worldwide send off of "I'm Lovin' It" in 2003. Initiated by the snappy jingle formed by Pharrell Williams, the mission expected to make a widespread and positive relationship with the McDonald's insight. The utilization of the motto across different media stages, from TV to computerized, further built up the brand's worldwide reach and social importance.

Computerized showcasing turned into a point of convergence for McDonald's in the 21st hundred years. The organization embraced web-based stages and online entertainment to draw in with buyers continuously. The send off of the "Our Food. Your Inquiries." crusade in 2014 exemplified McDonald's obligation to straightforwardness. The mission welcomed clients to pose any inquiries about McDonald's food, addressing fantasies and confusions while showing a readiness to participate in transparent correspondence.

The period of advanced promoting likewise saw the presentation of intuitive and customized encounters. McDonald's utilized versatile applications, internet requesting, and unwaveringness projects to upgrade client commitment. The McFlurry Creator application, presented in 2018, permitted clients to tweak their McFlurry pastries by picking their favored fixings and flavors. This intuitive methodology lined up with the pattern towards customized and vivid brand encounters.

Social obligation turned into a vital subject in McDonald's showcasing systems because of changing buyer assumptions. The organization zeroed in on imparting its obligation to supportability, moral obtaining, and local area commitment. Advertising messages featured drives, for example, the utilization of enclosure free eggs, reasonable fishing practices, and backing for neighborhood networks. This change in informing mirrored McDonald's familiarity with the developing significance of corporate obligation in forming shopper discernments.

McDonald's additionally perceived the force of wistfulness in advertising. The organization decisively once again introduced well known menu things from an earlier time, for example, the McRib or the Szechuan Sauce, gaining by clients' affectionate recollections and making a feeling of sentimentality. This approach not just taken advantage of the profound association that clients had with the brand yet in addition created buzz and energy around restricted time contributions.

One of the most prominent late promoting advancements was McDonald's co-operation with well known specialists and VIPs. Restricted version dinners organized by artists and powerhouses, for example, the Travis Scott Feast and the BTS Dinner, produced tremendous virtual entertainment buzz and drove pedestrian activity to McDonald's areas. These joint efforts showed McDonald's capacity to adjust its showcasing procedures to line up with contemporary mainstream society drifts and benefit from the impact of online entertainment.

McDonald's excursion into mainstream society has been impelled by a progression of imaginative showcasing and publicizing procedures. From the presentation of the Brilliant Curves as a visual identifier to the formation of paramount characters, trademarks, and missions, McDonald's has reliably adjusted its showcasing ways to deal with remain socially important. The organization's capacity to use associations, embrace computerized stages, convey social obligation, and tap into wistfulness highlights its deftness in answering changing buyer scenes. As McDonald's keeps on exploring the steadily developing elements of the cheap food industry and mainstream society, its promoting developments will without a doubt assume a focal part in forming the brand's story and keeping up with its status as a worldwide social symbol.

4.3 The first steps towards international expansion

The most vital moves towards worldwide development denoted a huge part in the advancement of McDonald's from a provincial example of overcoming adversity to a worldwide cheap food force to be reckoned with. As the brand acquired a fortification in the US during the 1950s and 1960s, the visionaries behind McDonald's perceived the undiscovered capacity past American lines. This account dives into the early attacks of McDonald's into worldwide business sectors, analyzing the difficulties, methodologies, and urgent minutes that laid the basis for its worldwide impression.

Beam Kroc, the instrumental figure in the public development of Mcdonald's, held onto a dream that stretched out a long ways past the boundaries of the US. The outcome of the establishment model, with its accentuation on functional proficiency and normalized processes, established a powerful starting point for taking the McDonald's idea worldwide. Kroc's desire was to make a brand that rose above social limits and turned into an image of quick, solid, and predictable feasting encounters around the world.

The main huge step towards worldwide extension occurred in 1967 with the launch of a McDonald's café in Richmond, English Columbia, Canada. While geologically near the US, this obvious McDonald's entrance into a market with an unmistakable social personality. The eatery's outcome in Canada highlighted the versatility of the McDonald's model to different shopper inclinations and made ready for additional extension past public boundaries.

Canada filled in as a proving ground, however McDonald's actual jump onto the worldwide stage happened with the kickoff of a café in Tokyo, Japan, in 1971. The decision of Japan as the primary non-English-talking country for McDonald's extension was vital. The Japanese market introduced a remarkable arrangement of difficulties, from contrasts in taste inclinations to newness to the idea of cheap food. In any case, McDonald's moved toward the Japanese market with a guarantee to understanding and adjusting to nearby traditions.

The outcome of McDonald's in Japan was not quick, and the organization confronted starting suspicion. The idea of cheap food, described by speedy help and normalized contributions, was novel in a culture that generally esteemed fastidious planning and scrupulousness. McDonald's explored these difficulties by presenting restricted menu things, like the Teriyaki Burger, and adjusting its functional model to line up with Japanese assumptions.

The way to deal with restriction turned into a foundation of McDonald's worldwide extension technique. Perceiving that shopper inclinations fluctuated across societies, McDonald's embraced "thinking worldwide, acting nearby." This implied fitting menus to suit neighborhood tastes, integrating territorial flavors, and regarding social responsive qualities. The progress of the confined methodology in Japan set a trend for McDonald's venture into different worldwide business sectors.

The 1970s saw McDonald's wandering into Europe, denoting a critical achievement in its worldwide development. The primary European McDonald's opened in Munich, Germany, in 1971, trailed by areas in the Netherlands and Britain. The

European development introduced a novel arrangement of difficulties, as McDonald's adjusted to different culinary customs, dialects, and social subtleties. However, the center standards of functional effectiveness and normalized processes stayed vital to McDonald's character.

As McDonald's extended across Europe, it confronted contest from laid out neighborhood restaurants as well as from assumptions about American inexpensive food. The organization answered by underscoring the nature of its fixings, the tidiness of its cafés, and a pledge to neighborhood networks. McDonald's tried to dissipate generalizations and position itself as a brand that embraced social variety while conveying a predictable and pleasant eating experience.

The 1980s saw McDonald's venture into Latin America, the Center East, and Asia-Pacific locales. The organization kept on refining its methodology of adjusting to neighborhood tastes while keeping a worldwide brand picture. In Latin America, McDonald's presented menu things like the McHuevo in Uruguay and the McArabia in the Center East. The local transformations stretched out past menu contributions to envelop eatery configuration, showcasing messages, and local area commitment.

The way to deal with global development was not without challenges. McDonald's confronted fights and opposition in certain districts, with worries going from social dominion to the apparent effect on neighborhood eats less. Accordingly, McDonald's effectively drawn in with nearby networks, addressing concerns and adjusting its systems to line up with social standards. The organization's obligation to corporate obligation and local area inclusion became basic to its worldwide extension story.

During the 1990s, McDonald's extended its presence in Asia, with a specific spotlight on China. The passage into the Chinese market, with the kickoff of the principal McDonald's in Shenzhen in 1990, denoted a critical second. China, with its rich culinary practices and tremendous customer market, presented both gigantic open doors and complex difficulties. McDonald's perceived the requirement for a patient and nuanced way to deal with win the hearts of Chinese purchasers.

The transformation to the Chinese market included menu restriction as well as a cautious thought of social subtleties. McDonald's integrated components of Chinese culture into its cafés, celebrated customary celebrations, and effectively took part in local area drives. The organization's progress in China exhibited its capacity to explore different social scenes and secure itself as a brand that regarded and embraced neighborhood values.

The 21st century carried new aspects to McDonald's global development procedures, driven by innovative progressions and changing buyer ways of behaving. The ascent of the web and virtual entertainment required a shift towards computerized promoting and online commitment. McDonald's embraced these changes, utilizing advanced stages to associate with purchasers, advance confined contributions, and accumulate continuous input.

Computerized advancements additionally affected the client experience, with the presentation of self-administration stands, versatile requesting, and conveyance administrations. These headways were receptive to developing buyer inclinations as well as mirrored McDonald's obligation to remaining at the cutting edge of innovation. The worldwide execution of these advanced arrangements displayed McDonald's capacity to adjust its functional model to line up with contemporary patterns.

The mid 2000s saw McDonald's exploring difficulties connected with wellbeing insights and changing dietary inclinations. Accordingly, the organization presented better menu choices, like servings of mixed greens, barbecued chicken, and natural product cuts. The accentuation on menu expansion expected to take special care of a more extensive scope of buyer tastes while tending to worries about the nourishing substance of inexpensive food.

McDonald's kept on fortifying its obligation to corporate obligation and supportability as necessary parts of its worldwide image personality. The organization vowed to utilize just enclosure free eggs, focused on supportable obtaining rehearses, and zeroed in on lessening its ecological effect. These drives were vital reactions to cultural assumptions as well as lined up with McDonald's vision of being a capable and scrupulous worldwide resident.

The continuous excursion of McDonald's into worldwide business sectors is described by a mix of globalization and restriction. The organization's capacity to offset normalized functional cycles with a receptiveness to assorted societies and buyer inclinations has been instrumental in its worldwide achievement. McDonald's stands as a demonstration of the possibility that a brand can rise above geological limits while regarding and adjusting to the uniqueness of each market it enters.

The most vital moves towards worldwide extension were crucial minutes in McDonald's direction from a territorial cheap food chain to a worldwide social symbol. The organization's capacity to explore the intricacies of different business sectors, adjust to social subtleties, and keep a pledge to functional greatness established the groundwork for its getting through worldwide presence. McDonald's initial endeavors into Canada, Japan, Europe, and past set up for an excursion that keeps on developing, mirroring the unique transaction among globalization and restriction in the cheap food industry.

Chapter 5

Trials and Triumphs

The excursion of Mcdonald's, similar to any worldwide undertaking, has been set apart by a progression of preliminaries and wins — challenges that tried versatility and developments impelled its prosperity. From the beginning of its commencement to its ongoing status as a worldwide social symbol, McDonald's has endured storms and celebrated triumphs. This story investigates the preliminaries and wins that have characterized McDonald's advancement throughout the long term.

Preliminaries:

Early Mishaps and Transformation:

Mcdonald's, in its beginning years, confronted its portion of difficulties. The progress from a nearby outcome in San Bernardino to a public and later global peculiarity was not without obstacles. One of the early misfortunes was the need to adjust to new business sectors and purchaser assumptions. The confined outcome of the first McDonald's in California didn't ensure prompt acknowledgment in different locales. The organization needed to explore various societies, tastes, and administrative conditions, requiring a steady course of transformation and learning.

Functional Difficulties:

The very rules that made McDonald's effective — functional productivity, normalization, and speed — likewise presented difficulties. Keeping up with consistency across huge number of establishments overall required fastidious oversight. Functional difficulties, including inventory network the board, quality control, and staffing, tried the organization's capacity to maintain its principles. Cases of functional hiccups, whether as production network interruptions or quality worries, became crucial points in time requesting quick goal and harm control.

Advertising Issues:

Mcdonald's, as a universally perceived brand, has been defenseless to advertising difficulties. Wellbeing concerns connected with inexpensive food, moral obtaining rehearses, and natural effect have been subjects of examination. Advertising emergencies, for example, debates over the healthful substance of McDonald's contributions, moved the organization to address advancing cultural assumptions. The need to explore these issues while keeping up with shopper trust expected vital correspondence and a guarantee to straightforwardness.

Changing Shopper Inclinations:

The cheap food scene has gone through huge changes throughout the long term, driven by changing shopper inclinations. The ascent of wellbeing cognizance, an interest for more different menu choices, and a rising spotlight on supportability presented difficulties for Mcdonald's. Adjusting to moving purchaser patterns without compromising the center brand character of helpful and reasonable inexpensive food turned into a sensitive difficult exercise. The organization confronted the preliminary of remaining significant in a climate where purchaser assumptions were developing quickly.

Wins:

Worldwide Development and Normalization:

One of McDonald's initial victories was its effective venture into worldwide business sectors. The organization's capacity to imitate its functional model internationally, keeping a normalized and reliable experience, displayed the strength of its establishment framework. The Brilliant Curves turned into an image of a neighborhood cheap food joint as well as of a worldwide brand. McDonald's shown the way that it could rise above social contrasts while maintaining its obligation to effectiveness and quality.

Creative Showcasing Systems:

McDonald's has been a pioneer in the domain of showcasing, and its imaginative systems stand apart as wins in building a worldwide brand. The presentation of notable missions like "Search for the Brilliant Curves" and characters like Ronald McDonald made an enduring engraving in mainstream society. The "I'm Lovin' It" crusade during the 2000s, with its snappy jingle and worldwide reverberation, further hardened McDonald's situation as a brand with a finger on the beat of purchaser opinion.

Restricted Variation:

McDonald's prevailed in its capacity to find some kind of harmony between worldwide consistency and neighborhood variation. Perceiving that shopper tastes shift broadly across societies, the organization embraced a system of "reasoning worldwide, acting neighborhood." The presentation of district explicit menu things, taking care of nearby culinary inclinations, turned into a victory of McDonald's confinement approach. From the McArabia in the Center East to the Matcha McFlurry in Japan, McDonald's exhibited its ability to reverberate with different palates.

Key Associations and Coordinated efforts:

McDonald's prosperity incorporates key associations and coordinated efforts that have pushed its image into new levels. The joint efforts with Disney, as found in the formation of the Blissful Dinner highlighting darling characters, represent how cooperative energies with other social symbols can prompt common victories. The essential coordinated efforts with famous performers and powerhouses, like the Travis Scott Feast and the BTS Dinner, supported deals as well as created gigantic buzz via web-based entertainment.

Advanced Change:

Embracing the computerized age has been a victory for Mcdonald's. The organization's effective reception of computerized advances, from portable requesting to self-administration stands, mirrors its nimbleness in answering changing customer ways of behaving. The computerized developments improved client accommodation as well as displayed McDonald's obligation to remaining at the front line of mechanical progressions. The "McDonald's Representing things to come" idea, highlighting modernized feasting regions and upgraded computerized encounters, is a demonstration of the brand's obligation to development.

Worldwide Social Symbol Status:

Maybe one of McDonald's most noteworthy victories is its status as a worldwide social symbol. The Brilliant Curves, at first intended for a nearby eatery in California, have turned into a generally perceived image of cheap food. McDonald's has risen above its beginnings to turn into a portrayal of American culture and private enterprise. Its presence in films, writing, workmanship, and ordinary discussions verifies its social importance and win in laying out a brand that resounds around the world.

Corporate Obligation and Manageability:

In a period where corporate obligation is examined, McDonald's victories in its obligation to manageability and social obligation. Promises to utilize confine free eggs, supportable obtaining rehearses, and natural drives grandstand a proactive way to deal with tending to cultural worries. McDonald's perceived that being a dependable corporate resident isn't simply an ethical objective yet in addition an essential victory in building entrust with an undeniably faithful customer base.

The preliminaries and wins of McDonald's have shaped its story, making a dynamic and strong brand that has persevered for a really long time. From the difficulties of entering new business sectors to the imaginative showcasing procedures that have imbued McDonald's in mainstream society, every preliminary has been met with an essential victory. As McDonald's keeps on developing in light of an always impacting world, its capacity to explore difficulties and profit by amazing open doors will without out a doubt shape the following sections of its worldwide excursion.

5.1 The ups and downs of McDonald's journey through the 1960s

The 1960s was a critical 10 years throughout the entire existence of Mcdonald's, set apart by huge high points and low points that molded the direction of the notable cheap food chain. This period saw the organization change from a fruitful provincial dare to a prospering public and worldwide peculiarity. The promising and less promising times of McDonald's excursion during the 1960s mirror the difficulties of development, the rise of key developments, and the foundation of an establishment for future achievement.

Ups:

Public Diversifying and Beam Kroc's Vision:

One of the characterizing ups of McDonald's during the 1960s was the public diversifying methodology initiated by Beam Kroc. Kroc, a visionary business person, perceived the undiscovered possibility of the McDonald's idea past its unique area in San Bernardino, California. In 1954, Kroc went into an establishment concurrence with the McDonald siblings, Dick and Macintosh, and put into high gear an arrangement to bring the proficient and normalized McDonald's model to the other US. The launch of the first diversified McDonald's in Quite a while Plaines, Illinois, in 1955 denoted the start of the organization's public development.

Kroc's vision reached out past simply selling burgers; he intended to make a brand that represented consistency, speed, and quality across each McDonald's area. The ups of the 1960s lay in Kroc's tenacious quest for this vision. The establishment model worked with fast extension as well as established the groundwork for the worldwide achievement that McDonald's would accomplish in the next many years.

Advancements in Functional Effectiveness:

The 1960s saw earth shattering developments in McDonald's functional model, underscoring effectiveness and normalization. The execution of the "Speedee Administration Framework" denoted a huge up, smoothing out kitchen tasks and changing the cheap food industry. This framework presented the idea of sequential construction system creation in the kitchen, guaranteeing speedy and steady planning of food things. The emphasis on speed turned into a sign of the McDonald's image, separating it from conventional eat in cafés.

The presentation of the famous "Brilliant Curves" additionally happened during this period. Planned by modeler Stanley Meston, the Brilliant Curves turned into a visual identifier for McDonald's cafés. The essential utilization of the curves pointed at structural qualification as well as at making a generally unmistakable image. The Brilliant Curves, alongside the red and yellow variety plot, added to the formation of a strong brand picture that rose above individual areas.

Presentation of Essential Promoting:

The 1960s denoted the presentation of essential promoting systems that assumed a significant part in McDonald's turning into a commonly recognized name. The "Search for the Brilliant Curves" crusade, sent off in 1960, urged buyers to connect the curves with a solid and natural feasting experience. This mission, with its infectious jingle, underlined the visual acknowledgment of the Brilliant Curves as a directing image driving clients to Mcdonald's. The mission's prosperity showed McDonald's initial comprehension of the force of showcasing and forming buyer behavior potential.

Venture into Global Business sectors:

While most of McDonald's development during the 1960s zeroed in on the US, the ten years laid the basis for worldwide extension. The principal attack past U.S. borders happened in 1967 with the kickoff of a McDonald's café in Richmond,

English Columbia, Canada. In spite of the fact that Canada was geologically close, this move denoted the start of McDonald's worldwide desires. The outcome in Canada exhibited the flexibility of the McDonald's model to global business sectors and set up for additional extensive worldwide endeavors in the next many years.

Downs:

Franchisee-Driven Clashes:

The quick extension of McDonald's through diversifying was not without challenges, and the 1960s saw clashes between the organization and some franchisees. As McDonald's developed, strains emerged over issues, for example, sovereignty charges, command over menus, and conflicts on functional rules. Some franchisees felt that the organization's push for consistency and normalization restricted their independence and blocked their capacity to take care of nearby preferences. These struggles prompted fights in court and stressed connections among McDonald's and a group of its franchisees.

Beam Kroc, while instrumental in the public diversifying system, confronted difficulties in keeping a fragile harmony between corporate control and franchisee fulfillment. The downs of the 1960s included examples where franchisees opposed specific corporate mandates, featuring the intricacies innate in dealing with a quickly extending establishment organization.

Changes in Purchaser Discernments:

As McDonald's turned into an omnipresent presence in American people group, the 1960s likewise saw shifts in buyer view of cheap food. A few pundits raised worries about the dietary substance and wellbeing ramifications of cheap food contributions. Mcdonald's, alongside other cheap food chains, confronted investigation over the effect of its items on general wellbeing. While the disadvantages of changing buyer discernments were not one of a kind to Mcdonald's, the organization needed to explore developing cultural mentalities toward diet and nourishment.

Lawful and Administrative Difficulties:

The 1960s brought lawful and administrative difficulties for Mcdonald's, mirroring the organization's rising noticeable quality. The downs included fights over drafting guidelines, for certain networks opposing the section of McDonald's eateries because of worries about traffic, commotion, and stylish contemplations. Because of these difficulties, McDonald's needed to take part in fights in court to affirm working in specific locations right. These lawful and administrative issues featured the strains between the quick extension of cheap food chains and the interests of neighborhood networks.

Rivalry and Market Immersion:

As McDonald's developed, it confronted expanded contest from other inexpensive food chains entering the market. The disadvantages incorporated the difficulties of keeping up with piece of the pie in a climate where contenders were competing for a similar purchaser base. Market immersion in specific locales likewise introduced obstacles, requiring McDonald's to investigate new roads for development and development to remain ahead in a cutthroat scene.

Advertising Misfortunes:

The potential gains of McDonald's promoting drives were incidentally joined by advertising mishaps. During the 1960s, the organization confronted reactions connected with its promoting rehearses, with worries raised about the focusing of kids and the possible effect on dietary propensities. These evaluates foreshadowed later discussions about the impact of inexpensive food promoting on general wellbeing. While these drawbacks didn't fundamentally imprint McDonald's development, they denoted the start of a pattern where the organization's showcasing practices would go under expanded investigation.

The 1960s embodied an extraordinary period in McDonald's set of experiences, portrayed by eminent promising and less promising times. The ten years saw the public diversifying technique flourish, developments in functional productivity, and the presentation of significant showcasing efforts. At the same time, McDonald's experienced difficulties connected with franchisee clashes, moving customer discernments, fights in court, expanded contest, and periodic advertising misfortunes.

The ups of the 1960s laid the preparation for the brand's worldwide achievement, while the downs highlighted the intricacies of dealing with a quickly extending and powerful cheap food realm. As McDonald's explored the complexities of development and transformation during the 1960s, it set up for the proceeded with advancement of the brand in the many years that followed.

5.2 Kroc's leadership style and management challenges

Beam Kroc's authority style and the administration challenges he confronted were instrumental in forming the direction of McDonald's from a territorial accomplishment to a worldwide peculiarity. Kroc, frequently alluded to as the "pioneer" of McDonald's Organization, assumed a focal part in the organization's development, functional developments, and the foundation of a universally perceived brand. This story investigates Kroc's initiative style, the difficulties he experienced, and the procedures he utilized to explore the intricacies of dealing with a quickly developing and powerful cheap food domain.

Authority Style:

Innovative Vision:

At the center of Beam Kroc's authority was an enterprising vision that stretched out a long ways past the first McDonald's café in San Bernardino, California. Kroc, a multi-blender milkshake machine deals specialist, found the little yet fruitful San Bernardino eatery run by the McDonald siblings in 1954. Perceiving the possibility to duplicate its prosperity on a public and worldwide scale, Kroc went into an establishment concurrence with the McDonald siblings and set out on an excursion to change McDonald's into a worldwide brand.

Kroc's enterprising soul was portrayed by an intense and aggressive vision. He saw McDonald's as an assortment of individual cafés as well as a normalized and reliable eating experience that could be reproduced around the world. His prescience in perceiving the versatility of the establishment model established the groundwork for McDonald's remarkable development.

Obligation to Functional Greatness:

Kroc's authority style accentuated functional proficiency and normalization. He had faith in conveying a steady encounter to clients, regardless of which McDonald's they visited. The presentation of the "Speedee Administration Framework" was a demonstration of this responsibility. This framework reformed the kitchen tasks, underlining velocity and accuracy in the readiness of food things. Kroc comprehended the significance of smoothing out cycles to guarantee fast help — an essential rule that became inseparable from the McDonald's image.

Kroc's devotion to functional greatness stretched out to each part of the business. From the plan of eateries to the format of kitchen hardware, he tried to make a framework that could be imitated with accuracy. The objective was to guarantee that a client in California had a similar encounter as a client in New York or Tokyo.

Showcasing Developments and Brand Building:

One more aspect of Kroc's administration style was his imaginative way to deal with advertising and brand building. During the 1960s, he sent off the "Search for the Brilliant Curves" crusade, underscoring the visual acknowledgment of McDonald's cafés. The utilization of vital jingles and famous characters like Ronald McDonald added to the formation of a brand that rose above individual areas. Kroc grasped the force of promoting in forming buyer discernments and building unwaveringness.

Under Kroc's initiative, McDonald's turned into a trailblazer in utilizing promoting to make areas of strength for a personality. The famous Brilliant Curves, planned by designer Stanley Meston, turned into an image of inexpensive food and a visual anchor for the brand. Kroc's promoting developments assumed a significant part in laying out McDonald's as a commonly recognized name and a social symbol.

Flexibility and Globalization:

Kroc's authority style exhibited flexibility to changing conditions and a receptiveness to globalization. As McDonald's extended past U.S. borders, Kroc perceived the requirement for confinement. The system of "reasoning worldwide, acting nearby" became basic to McDonald's global achievement. Kroc comprehended that customer tastes changed across societies, and he energized the variation of menus to suit neighborhood inclinations.

The receptiveness to globalization was clear in McDonald's entrance into different worldwide business sectors, including Japan, Europe, Latin America, and Asia-Pacific districts. Kroc's initiative worked with the foundation of McDonald's as a worldwide brand, fit for adjusting to the subtleties of various business sectors while keeping a center character.

The executives Difficulties:

Fast Extension and Franchisee Relations:

One of the critical administration challenges Kroc confronted was the quick development of McDonald's through diversifying. While the establishment model was fundamental for accomplishing public and worldwide reach, it brought difficulties connected with franchisee relations. As the quantity of establishments developed, strains emerged over issues, for example, eminence charges, command over menus, and functional rules.

Dealing with a tremendous organization of franchisees expected Kroc to work out some kind of harmony between corporate control and franchisee fulfillment. Some franchisees opposed specific corporate mandates, feeling that the push for consistency restricted their independence. Kroc needed to address these worries while guaranteeing that the center standards of functional proficiency and normalization were maintained across the establishment organization.

Functional Control and Quality Affirmation:

Keeping up with functional control and guaranteeing reliable quality across large number of McDonald's areas introduced continuous difficulties. Kroc's obligation to normalization confronted the trial of functional varieties and expected quality irregularities. The test was not exclusively to lay out severe functional rules yet additionally to execute compelling quality affirmation measures.

Kroc carried out thorough preparation projects to guarantee that franchisees stuck to McDonald's functional norms. Notwithstanding, the decentralized idea of the establishment model implied that keeping up with consistency required persistent oversight. The test of finding some kind of harmony between corporate control and the independence of individual franchisees persevered as McDonald's extended its impression.

Lawful and Administrative Obstacles:

The developing conspicuousness of McDonald's brought legitimate and administrative difficulties. The organization confronted drafting fights, for certain networks opposing the section of McDonald's eateries because of worries about traffic, commotion, and stylish contemplations. Kroc needed to explore legitimate obstacles to affirm the organization's on the whole correct to work in specific areas.

Administrative difficulties likewise arose concerning issues like sanitation principles, publicizing practices, and work guidelines. Kroc had to oversee legitimate illicit relationships and administrative consistence on a public and global scale, adjusting McDonald's practices to line up with shifting lawful systems.

Changing Purchaser Discernments and Wellbeing Concerns:

As McDonald's turned into a prevailing power in the cheap food industry, changing purchaser discernments introduced difficulties. The 1960s saw a change in cultural perspectives towards diet and wellbeing, with worries raised about the wholesome substance and wellbeing ramifications of cheap food contributions. Kroc needed to explore the developing scene of shopper assumptions while keeping up with McDonald's allure.

The test of tending to wellbeing concerns turned out to be more articulated in later many years, however the seeds were planted during the 1960s. Kroc confronted the undertaking of answering changing purchaser feelings and proactively addressing reactions connected with the effect of inexpensive food on general wellbeing.

Rivalry and Market Immersion:

The serious scene acted administration challenges for Kroc like McDonald's extended. While the establishment model worked with quick development, it additionally implied that other inexpensive food chains could enter the market with comparable speed. Kroc needed to devise systems to keep up with piece of the pie and maintain McDonald's situation as an industry chief.

Market immersion in specific locales represented extra difficulties. Kroc expected to investigate new roads for development, whether through menu advancements, promoting systems, or the investigation of undiscovered business sectors. The test was to remain ahead in a dynamic and serious climate.

Systems and Arrangements:

Franchisee Joint effort and Preparing Projects:

To address difficulties connected with franchisee relations and functional control, Kroc executed cooperative drives. He perceived the significance of cultivating areas of strength for a with franchisees and including them in dynamic cycles. Cooperative endeavors, for example, the foundation of the Franchisee Warning Committee during the 1960s, gave a stage to correspondence and input.

Kroc likewise executed broad preparation projects to guarantee that franchisees and their staff stuck to McDonald's functional norms. The accentuation on preparing meant to ingrain a feeling of responsibility and obligation to the McDonald's image across the whole establishment organization.

Promoting and Brand Situating:

Kroc's way to deal with promoting and brand building assumed a urgent part in conquering difficulties connected with changing buyer discernments. The imaginative promoting efforts, including the "Search for the Brilliant Curves" and the presentation of famous characters like Ronald McDonald, added to molding a positive brand picture. Kroc's promoting techniques pointed at drawing in clients as well as at imparting a feeling of trust and commonality.

To address worries about wellbeing and nourishment, McDonald's subsequently presented better menu choices, showing a responsiveness to changing purchaser inclinations. Kroc's obligation to adjusting the menu while saving the center character of McDonald's displayed an essential way to deal with tending to cultural worries.

Restriction Techniques for Global Business sectors:

Because of difficulties related with globalization, Kroc embraced limitation methodologies. He comprehended that a one-size-fits-all approach wouldn't work in different global business sectors. Kroc supported the transformation of menus to suit nearby preferences, integrating territorial flavors and regarding social responsive qualities.

The progress of McDonald's in worldwide business sectors, for example, Japan, showed the viability of this limitation approach. Kroc's eagerness to tailor the McDonald's insight to line up with nearby inclinations added to the brand's acknowledgment and accomplishment on a worldwide scale.

Advancement and Enhancement:

To handle difficulties connected with contest and market immersion, Kroc embraced development and expansion. McDonald's presented menu developments, for example, the Large Macintosh during the 1960s, to keep the contributions new and interesting to an expansive client base. The accentuation on presenting very interesting menu things turned into a methodology to separate McDonald's from rivals.

Kroc additionally investigated broadening past the center menu, wandering into breakfast things and sweets. The presentation of the Filet-O-Fish in light of territorial inclinations exhibited McDonald's flexibility to assorted preferences. These essential moves meant to keep up with client premium and counter the difficulties presented by market immersion.

Corporate Obligation and Local area Commitment:

Tending to legitimate and administrative moves expected a proactive way to deal with corporate obligation and local area commitment. Kroc perceived the significance of being a dependable corporate resident, effectively captivating with nearby networks and tending to worries. McDonald's focused on drives like the Ronald McDonald House Noble cause, exhibiting a guarantee to social obligation.

This people group driven approach not just assisted in building positive associations with neighborhood networks yet additionally added to McDonald's picture as a brand that thought often about the prosperity of the spots it worked in. Kroc's initiative underscored the significance of corporate obligation as a vital part of McDonald's personality.

Inheritance and Proceeded with Effect:

Beam Kroc's initiative style and his systems to address the executives challenges made a permanent imprint on McDonald's and the cheap food industry overall. His pioneering vision changed McDonald's from a neighborhood example of overcoming adversity to a worldwide social symbol. The accentuation on functional greatness, promoting advancements, flexibility to globalization, and key answers for the board difficulties molded the establishment for McDonald's persevering through progress.

Kroc's inheritance reaches out past the business domain to the social scene. The Brilliant Curves turned into an image of inexpensive food and an indispensable piece of mainstream society.

The advancements presented under his administration, from the Speedee Administration Framework to notable showcasing efforts, set benchmarks for the business. Mcdonald's, as a brand, mirrors Kroc's vision of conveying a reliable and pleasant feasting experience to clients around the world.

While Kroc confronted difficulties inborn in dealing with a quickly extending establishment organization, his capacity to explore intricacies and carry out successful arrangements laid the preparation for McDonald's supported development. The techniques he utilized, whether in franchisee joint effort, showcasing, globalization, or corporate obligation, keep on impacting McDonald's activities and the more extensive cheap food scene.

Beam Kroc's initiative style and the board techniques during the early stages of McDonald's assumed a significant part in forming the brand's character and worldwide achievement. The highs and lows of this excursion, from the provokes of fast development to the advancements that characterized Mcdonald's, mirror the unique idea of Kroc's administration. As McDonald's keeps on advancing, Kroc's heritage stays implanted in the organization's DNA, highlighting the getting through effect of his visionary way to deal with administration and the executives.

5.3 Key moments that tested the resilience of the franchise

The flexibility of the McDonald's establishment has been tried all through its celebrated history by a progression of key minutes, each provoking the organization to adjust, develop, and defeat impediments. These significant crossroads have molded McDonald's as a worldwide brand as well as exhibited its capacity to explore a powerful business scene. From financial slumps to shifts in shopper inclinations, the establishment has endured storms and arisen more grounded. This story investigates key minutes that tried the strength of the McDonald's establishment, featuring the techniques utilized to defeat difficulties and proceed with its direction as an inexpensive food monster.

1. **Financial Difficulties during the 1970s:**
   The 1970s presented financial difficulties universally, with variables, for example, expansion and oil emergencies influencing organizations. Mcdonald's, as a conspicuous player in the cheap food industry, confronted the double test of rising working expenses and changing customer ways of managing money. The organization's strength during this period was clear in its essential reactions.

   To relieve the effect of expansion, McDonald's executed cost increments yet in addition zeroed in on cost efficiencies inside its activities. The presentation of the "E-Z Framework," a high level mechanized administration framework, helped upgrade functional proficiency and control costs. This mechanical development exhibited McDonald's versatility as well as laid the basis for future progressions in eatery the board frameworks.

   Besides, McDonald's differentiated its menu to take care of changing buyer inclinations. The presentation of the Egg McMuffin in 1972 denoted an introduction to the morning meal market, giving an effective answer for the financial difficulties. By widening its contributions, McDonald's shown flexibility notwithstanding monetary headwinds and a promise to meeting developing buyer needs.

2. **Presentation of the Chicken McNugget (1983):**
   The mid 1980s achieved a urgent second for McDonald's with the presentation

of the Chicken McNugget. This creative item extended the menu as well as addressed an essential reaction to the changing scene of inexpensive food inclinations. The Chicken McNugget's prosperity featured McDonald's capacity to adjust to moving buyer tastes and benefit from arising food patterns.

The flexibility exhibited at this time was tied in with presenting another item as well as about figuring out the significance of expansion. The Chicken McNugget turned into a social peculiarity, contributing essentially to McDonald's primary concern. This essential move exhibited the establishment's ability to improve and remain important in the cutthroat cheap food market.

3. **Answering Wellbeing Concerns and Evolving Diets (2000s):**
The 2000s denoted a time of expanded public mindfulness with respect to wellbeing and sustenance, prompting changing buyer inclinations. McDonald's confronted examination over the wholesome substance of its contributions, and the establishment needed to answer worries about cheap food's effect on general wellbeing. This second tried McDonald's flexibility in tending to cultural moves and keeping up with its market position.

Because of wellbeing concerns, McDonald's found a way proactive ways to offer better menu choices. The presentation of servings of mixed greens, natural product cuts, and different choices displayed a pledge to adjusting to changing buyer requests. The "Go Dynamic!" feast, embraced by wellness symbol Oprah Winfrey, planned to situate McDonald's as an ally of better ways of life. The establishment's capacity to answer wellbeing cognizant shoppers exhibited strength despite advancing cultural assumptions.

4. **Supersize Me Narrative (2004):**
The arrival of the narrative "Supersize Me" in 2004 introduced a huge test to McDonald's public picture. The film, which recorded movie producer Morgan Spurlock's extended analysis of devouring just McDonald's food, raised worries about the dietary substance and wellbeing ramifications of cheap food. The narrative turned into a point of convergence for banters on diet, weight, and the cheap food industry's job in general wellbeing.

McDonald's answered the test presented by "Supersize Me" through a mix of promoting and functional changes. The establishment got rid of the "Supersize" choice from its menu and presented better other options. Also, McDonald's participated in advertising endeavors to impart its obligation to giving dietary data and supporting better decisions. This second tried McDonald's capacity to explore negative exposure and highlighted the significance of straightforwardness and responsiveness in keeping up with buyer trust.

5. **Worldwide Financial Downturn (2008-2009):**
The worldwide financial downturn in 2008-2009 introduced a difficult business climate for some ventures, including cheap food. As shoppers confronted monetary vulnerabilities, there was a change in spending designs, with some deciding on more financially savvy feasting choices. McDonald's flexibility during this

financial slump was exemplified by its capacity to endure the hardship as well as flourish in testing conditions.

McDonald's essential reaction to the financial downturn included esteem centered promoting efforts, for example, the "Dollar Menu," which reverberated with thrifty customers. The establishment's accentuation on moderateness and worth situated it as an alluring choice during extreme monetary times. McDonald's shown versatility by utilizing its worth situated technique to keep up with and even develop its client base despite monetary difficulties.

6. **Ascent of Quick Easygoing Contenders (2010s):**

The 2010s saw the ascent of quick easygoing eating ideas, introducing a test to conventional cheap food chains. Purchasers, especially twenty to thirty year olds, looked for eating encounters that accentuated newness, quality fixings, and adjustable choices. This change in inclinations represented a possible danger to McDonald's market predominance and tried the establishment's capacity to stay significant in a changing culinary scene.

McDonald's answered the ascent of quick easygoing contenders by executing a progression of key drives. The "Make Your Taste" stage permitted clients to modify their burgers with various premium fixings. The presentation of the entire day breakfast and the McPick 2 advancement pointed toward giving more prominent adaptability and interesting to a different scope of customer inclinations. McDonald's versatility notwithstanding advancing rivalry lay in its ability to improve and present menu and administration upgrades that lined up with contemporary feasting patterns.

7. **Worldwide Pandemic and the Ascent of Conveyance (2020s):**

The beginning of the Coronavirus pandemic in the mid 2020s carried extraordinary difficulties to the café business, including Mcdonald's. Lockdowns, social separating measures, and changes in purchaser conduct required a quick variation to new conditions. The pandemic tried McDonald's strength on various fronts, from functional coherence to meeting the advancing necessities of clients.

McDonald's answered the difficulties presented by the pandemic by speeding up advanced change drives. The establishment put resources into contactless innovation, portable requesting, and conveyance administrations, giving clients advantageous and safe choices. The execution of drive-through improvements, curbside pickup, and the extension of McDelivery displayed McDonald's capacity to turn because of outside shocks.

Besides, the pandemic highlighted the significance of local area commitment and corporate obligation. McDonald's drives, for example, offering help to bleeding edge laborers and networks out of luck, showed a guarantee to cultural prosperity during testing times. McDonald's flexibility during the worldwide pandemic was portrayed by deftness, development, and a devotion to meeting the changing requirements of buyers in a phenomenal climate.

The key minutes that tried the strength of the McDonald's establishment over the course of the many years reflect the difficulties looked as well as the essential reactions that have characterized its getting through progress. From financial slumps to shifts in shopper inclinations and worldwide emergencies, McDonald's has exhibited a capacity to adjust, develop, and stay a forerunner in the cheap food industry.

The establishment's flexibility is well established in its obligation to functional greatness, advertising developments, versatility to changing customer requests, and key reactions to outer difficulties. Every snapshot of testing has turned into a chance for McDonald's to develop, improve, and reaffirm its situation as a worldwide brand.

As McDonald's keeps on exploring a consistently changing business scene, the examples gained from these key minutes act as an aide for future difficulties. The establishment's capacity to answer cultural assumptions, embrace innovative headways, and keep an emphasis on consumer loyalty highlights its flexibility and continuous effect on the inexpensive food industry. The excursion of Mcdonald's, set apart by these urgent minutes, is a demonstration of the persevering through strength and flexibility of one of the world's most famous establishments.

Chapter 6

Beyond Burgers and Fries

"Past Hamburgers and French fries: McDonald's Development in a Changing Culinary Scene"

In the steadily developing scene of the cheap food industry, McDonald's has confronted a progression of extraordinary difficulties that reach out a long ways past its notable hamburgers and French fries. As buyer inclinations shift, dietary patterns change, and cultural assumptions develop, McDonald's has explored an excursion of variation and development to stay a worldwide culinary monster. This story investigates the powerful development of McDonald's past its conventional contributions, digging into the organization's reaction to changing culinary scenes, arising food patterns, and the quest for a more different and comprehensive menu.

1. **Broadening of Menu Contributions:**
   While McDonald's begun as a cheeseburger stand during the 1940s, its development into a worldwide cheap food monster has been set apart by an essential expansion of menu contributions. In the early years, the menu was based on burgers, fries, and shakes. Nonetheless, as shopper tastes developed and requests for assortment expanded, McDonald's left on an excursion to extend its contributions.

   The presentation of the Filet-O-Fish during the 1960s was an early sign of McDonald's readiness to expand its menu to take care of various preferences and inclinations. This pattern went on over the course of the years with the expansion of things like Chicken McNuggets during the 1980s and the McFlurry during the 1990s. These menu extensions were receptive to changing buyer inclinations as well as displayed McDonald's capacity to enhance inside the bounds of the cheap food model.

   As of late, the organization has found a way further ways to expand its menu by integrating better choices. Mixed greens, natural product cuts, and different options were acquainted with address developing worries about nourishment and dietary decisions. The accentuation on expansion mirrors McDonald's obligation to giving a large number of decisions, guaranteeing that there is something for everybody on the menu.

2. **Embracing Wellbeing and Health:**

   The cultural shift towards wellbeing and health has essentially influenced the food business, and McDonald's has not been resistant to these evolving assumptions. As customers become more aware of their dietary decisions, the conventional picture of inexpensive food as unfortunate has provoked cheap food monsters like McDonald's to reconsider their way to deal with menu contributions.

   One of the crucial minutes in this shift towards wellbeing cognizance was McDonald's reaction to the narrative "Supersize Me" in 2004. The film featured the potential wellbeing gambles related with over the top cheap food utilization and provoked McDonald's to rethink its menu choices. The organization progressively eliminated the "Supersize" choice, presented better other options, and left on an excursion towards straightforwardness in showing dietary data.

   In later years, McDonald's has kept on investigating better choices and adjust to changing health patterns. The expansion of expense servings of mixed greens, barbecued chicken things, and the expulsion of counterfeit additives from a menu things highlight McDonald's obligation to meeting the developing assumptions for wellbeing cognizant purchasers. This essential turn towards wellbeing and health lines up with more extensive cultural patterns and exhibits McDonald's capacity to adjust to the changing scene of dietary inclinations.

3. **Answering Dietary Patterns:**

   The ascent of dietary patterns and inclinations, going from vegetarianism to plant-based counts calories, has introduced the two difficulties and potential open doors for Mcdonald's. Perceiving the developing interest for meat choices, the organization has decisively embraced these patterns by integrating plant-based choices into its menu.

   One prominent reaction to the flood in plant-based abstains from food is the presentation of the McPlant line as a team with Past Meat.

   McDonald's introduction to plant-based burgers and elective protein choices flags an acknowledgment of the moving dietary scene and the longing for more practical and moral food decisions. This move not just takes care of a more extensive scope of dietary inclinations yet in addition positions McDonald's as a player in the undeniably well known market for plant-based other options.

   The consideration of veggie lover and vegetarian choices in specific business sectors likewise mirrors McDonald's obligation to worldwide inclusivity. Adjusting to different dietary inclinations has turned into a vital part of the organization's methodology, permitting McDonald's to keep up with its importance in a period where purchasers look for more customized and shifted feasting encounters.

4. **Social Confinement:**

One of the signs of McDonald's worldwide achievement has been its capacity to adjust its menu to neighborhood tastes and social inclinations. The idea of social limitation perceives that buyer palates vary around the world, and what works in a single market may not be guaranteed to reverberate in another. McDonald's has reliably exhibited a pledge to fitting its contributions to suit the different culinary inclinations of different locales.

For instance, in India, where a critical piece of the populace follows a veggie lover diet, McDonald's has presented a variety of vegan choices, including the McAloo Tikki and the Veg Maharaja Macintosh. In Japan, McDonald's has highlighted things like the Teriyaki Burger, taking care of neighborhood flavor profiles. This obligation to social restriction grandstands McDonald's flexibility as well as improves its allure in various regions of the planet.

Besides, McDonald's has embraced restricted time contributions and occasional varieties that draw motivation from neighborhood cooking styles. This essential methodology gives a sign of approval for social variety as well as produces energy and expectation among clients. By mixing worldwide consistency with nearby customization, McDonald's has effectively situated itself as a brand that regards and embraces culinary variety.

5. **Innovation and Customization:**

In the time of innovation and personalization, McDonald's has utilized advanced developments to improve client encounters and proposition more prominent customization. The execution of self-request booths, versatile requesting applications, and computerized installment choices has altered the manner in which clients communicate with the brand. This tech-driven approach lines up with changing buyer ways of behaving as well as permits McDonald's to smooth out its tasks and adjust to the requests of an educated age.

The presentation of the "Make Your Taste" stage was a critical move towards customization, permitting clients to fabricate their own burgers with different premium fixings. This customized approach resounds with the advanced buyer who values decision and distinction. McDonald's utilization of innovation to work with customization mirrors a sharp comprehension of the developing assumptions for purchasers in a period where personalization is central.

Besides, innovation plays had an impact in improving comfort through drives, for example, versatile requesting and conveyance administrations. The execution of McDelivery and organizations with outsider conveyance suppliers have permitted McDonald's to satisfy the need for in a hurry and at-home feasting encounters. This tech-driven development takes special care of changing customer propensities as well as positions McDonald's as a brand at the front line of the computerized upset in the food business.

6. **Feasible Practices and Ecological Obligation:**

As worldwide familiarity with ecological issues develops, buyers are progressively searching out brands that show a pledge to reasonable practices. McDonald's has perceived the significance of natural obligation and has embraced drives to decrease its environmental impression.

One of the remarkable minutes in McDonald's maintainability process was the obligation to source 100 percent of visitor bundling from sustainable, reused, or guaranteed sources by 2025. This aggressive objective mirrors McDonald's commitment to limiting its natural effect and embracing a roundabout economy approach. Also, endeavors to decrease single-use plastics and carry out eco-accommodating bundling arrangements show the organization's responsiveness to developing natural worries.

McDonald's has additionally made strides towards feasible obtaining of fixings, accentuating the significance of capable agrarian practices. The presentation of Rainforest Union Confirmed espresso and responsibilities to reasonable hamburger obtaining feature McDonald's obligation to a more supportable and moral inventory network.

7. **Local area Commitment and Social Effect:**

As well as developing its menu and functional practices, McDonald's has perceived the significance of local area commitment and social effect. The organization's drives reach out past the limits of its cafés, showing a guarantee to having a constructive outcome in the networks it serves.

The foundation of the Ronald McDonald House Noble cause (RMHC) in 1974 was an essential second that displayed McDonald's devotion to supporting families during testing times. RMHC gives a usual hangout spot for families with wiped out youngsters getting clinical treatment, highlighting McDonald's obligation to social obligation and local area government assistance.

McDonald's has likewise participated in different local area based drives, including instructive projects, nearby sponsorships, and associations with beneficent associations. These endeavors feature the's comprehension brand might interpret its job as a corporate resident and its obligation to making a positive effect past the domain of cheap food.

The story of McDonald's past hamburgers and French fries is a story of variation, development, and responsiveness to a changing culinary scene. From broadening menu contributions to embracing wellbeing and health patterns, answering dietary inclinations, and utilizing innovation for customization, McDonald's has exhibited a momentous capacity to develop with the times.

The essential moves towards manageability, social restriction, and social effect highlight McDonald's obligation to being a mindful worldwide brand. As the organization keeps on exploring the powerful scene of the food business, these drives position McDonald's as a cheap food goliath as well as a brand that perceives its part in forming a more comprehensive, various, and practical culinary future.

In the consistently developing universe of cheap food, McDonald's excursion past hamburgers and French fries mirrors a pledge to meeting the different requirements and assumptions for its worldwide client base. As the culinary scene keeps on developing, McDonald's will probably confront new difficulties and open doors, and its capacity to enhance and adjust will be critical in forming its future direction in the steadily impacting universe of cheap food feasting.

6.1 Diversification and the introduction of new menu items

"Broadening and the Presentation of New Menu Things: McDonald's Culinary Development"

Mcdonald's, the notorious cheap food goliath, has gone through a huge culinary development throughout the long term, changing from a cheeseburger driven menu to a different exhibit of contributions that take special care of an expansive range of tastes and inclinations. The essential presentation of new menu things and a guarantee to broadening play had a crucial impact in McDonald's capacity to remain pertinent, appeal to changing buyer inclinations, and explore the unique scene of the cheap food industry. This story investigates the complex excursion of McDonald's in enhancing its menu, analyzing key minutes, creative augmentations, and the more extensive ramifications of this culinary advancement.

1. **Starting points and Early Menu:**
   McDonald's excursion into the universe of cheap food started during the 1940s with an emphasis on basic and direct contributions. The early menu was based on the basics - burgers, cheeseburgers, fries, and refreshments. The McDonald's siblings, Richard and Maurice, laid out a framework in view of productivity and speed, establishing the groundwork for the cheap food model. It was the point at which the idea of cheap food was inseparable from fast, reasonable, and tasty hamburgers and French fries.

   As McDonald's extended past its unique San Bernardino area and left on an establishment model under the initiative of Beam Kroc during the 1950s, the menu remained established in its burger legacy. The organization's initial achievement was based on the straightforwardness and consistency of its contributions, mirroring the overall taste inclinations of the period.

2. **The Filet-O-Fish: A Spearheading Expansion (1960s):**
   The 1960s denoted a huge defining moment in McDonald's culinary development with the presentation of the Filet-O-Fish. This spearheading expansion to the menu was not just a reaction to the Lenten season, during which numerous clients swore off eating meat, yet in addition an early showing of McDonald's versatility to different dietary requirements.

   The Filet-O-Fish, highlighting a breaded fish filet with tartar sauce and a cut of cheddar, exhibited McDonald's capacity to grow its contributions past the customary hamburger driven menu. This essential move expanded the allure of

McDonald's as well as started a trend for future developments that would take special care of a more different client base.

3. **Chicken McNuggets: Taking advantage of Poultry Ubiquity (1980s):**
   During the 1980s, McDonald's indeed made a notable expansion to its menu with the presentation of Chicken McNuggets. This undeniable a takeoff from the customary spotlight on burgers and featured McDonald's acknowledgment of the developing prevalence of chicken as a cheap food choice.

   Chicken McNuggets, scaled down bits of breaded and seared chicken, turned into a moment achievement, adding to McDonald's standing as a flexible cheap food supplier. This creative expansion exhibited McDonald's responsiveness to developing customer inclinations and showed an eagerness to enhance its menu past the bounds of the exemplary burger.

4. **The McFlurry and Pastry Development (1990s):**
   As McDonald's placed the 1990s, there was a developing accentuation on growing the pastry menu and presenting creative sweet treats. The presentation of the McFlurry, a mixed frozen yogurt dessert with different blend ins, addressed a critical move towards enhancing past customary inexpensive food contributions.

   The McFlurry not just spoke to clients with a sweet tooth yet additionally mirrored a more extensive industry pattern of lifting pastry choices in the cheap food scene. The progress of the McFlurry featured McDonald's capacity to take advantage of the advancing cravings of shoppers for liberal and fluctuated dessert decisions.

5. **Mixed greens and Solid Choices (2000s):**
   The 2000s denoted an essential time in the cheap food industry as cultural mentalities towards wellbeing and health started to impact buyer decisions. McDonald's answered these changing elements by integrating better choices into its menu. Mixed greens, including different greens, vegetables, and protein choices, turned into a noticeable expansion, giving clients options in contrast to the conventional cheap food charge.

   This time likewise saw McDonald's obligation to straightforwardness in wholesome data, mirroring a more extensive shift towards furnishing clients with the devices to settle on informed dietary decisions. The presentation of better menu choices exhibited McDonald's capacity to offset center contributions with decisions took special care of a more wellbeing cognizant shopper base.

6. **Premium Contributions and Connoisseur Burgers (2010s):**
   During the 2010s, McDonald's took one more jump forward in its culinary development by presenting premium contributions and connoisseur burgers. The send off of the "Mark Made" line, permitting clients to redo their burgers with great fixings, addressed an essential move towards raising the cheap food experience.

   The consideration of connoisseur burgers with different garnishes and flavors exhibited McDonald's obligation to giving a more complex and adjustable menu. This drive lined up with more extensive industry patterns, where cheap food affixes tried to raise their contributions to rival quick easygoing feasting foundations.

7. **Plant-Based Choices and the McPlant Line (2020s):**
The culinary development of McDonald's arrived at another achievement during the 2020s with the presentation of plant-based choices. Perceiving the developing fame of plant-based slims down and the interest for meat choices, McDonald's sent off the McPlant line, including plant-based burgers and other meatless choices.

This move not just mirrored McDonald's responsiveness to changing dietary inclinations yet in addition situated the organization as a player in the growing business sector for plant-based other options. The McPlant line displayed McDonald's obligation to maintainability and the acknowledgment of natural contemplations in menu improvement.

8. **Restricted Time Contributions and Occasional Varieties:**

Notwithstanding long-lasting menu augmentations, McDonald's has decisively utilized restricted time contributions and occasional varieties to keep its menu dynamic and locking in. These drives produce energy among clients as well as permit McDonald's to explore different avenues regarding new flavors, fixings, and culinary ideas.

Occasional varieties, like the presentation of the McRib during explicit periods, have become exceptionally expected occasions that drive client interest and traffic. Restricted time contributions, frequently highlighting one of a kind coordinated efforts or provincial strengths, permit McDonald's to feature its versatility and imagination in light of developing culinary patterns.

Culinary Development: An Impression of Shopper Patterns:
McDonald's culinary advancement is intrinsically attached to the always changing scene of customer inclinations, dietary patterns, and cultural assumptions. The essential presentation of new menu things reflects not exclusively McDonald's responsiveness to these shifts yet in addition its job as a pioneer inside the cheap food industry.

The broadening of the menu has been driven by a nuanced comprehension of buyer cravings for assortment, customization, and better choices. McDonald's has effectively explored the sensitive equilibrium of safeguarding its notable contributions while embracing culinary development to take care of a more different and knowing client base.

The organization's readiness to explore different avenues regarding flavors, fixings, and cooking procedures features a guarantee to remaining on the ball in the serious cheap food market. The culinary development of McDonald's fills in as a demonstration of its capacity to adjust and flourish in an industry that is in a steady condition of motion.

Culinary Advancement and Future Skylines:

As McDonald's proceeds with its culinary development, what's to come holds invigorating opportunities for new menu advancements and variations. The outcome of plant-based choices, connoisseur contributions, and treat developments highlights McDonald's capacity to expect and answer arising culinary patterns.

The essential methodology of McDonald's in differentiating its menu not just takes special care of a more extensive scope of shopper inclinations yet additionally positions the brand as a unique player in the worldwide food industry. The organization's continuous obligation to maintainability, wellbeing cognizant decisions, and culinary innovativeness mirrors a proactive position towards meeting the developing assumptions for the present purchasers.

McDonald's culinary development from its unassuming starting points to a different and dynamic menu is a convincing story of flexibility, advancement, and responsiveness to buyer patterns. The presentation of new menu things over the course of the years isn't just an impression of changing preferences however an essential development that keeps McDonald's at the front of the inexpensive food scene. As the culinary excursion unfurls, McDonald's will without a doubt proceed to rethink and lift the inexpensive food experience, mirroring the consistently developing nature of the business and the different preferences of its worldwide client base.

6.2 Innovations in service, including the drive-thru concept

"Advancements in Assistance: McDonald's and the Drive-through Transformation"

The tale of McDonald's isn't just about burgers, fries, and shakes; additionally about spearheading developments in assistance have changed the cheap food industry. At the front of these developments is the drive-through idea, a game-changing improvement that reclassified comfort and openness for a great many clients around the world. This story investigates the development of administration at Mcdonald's, with a particular spotlight on the origin and effect of the drive-through, close by other outstanding developments that have formed the organization's way to deal with client experience.

1. **Birth of the Speedee Administration Framework:**
   McDonald's excursion towards administration advancement can be followed back to its initial days with the foundation of the Speedee Administration Framework. Brought about by the McDonald siblings, Richard and Maurice, during the 1940s, this framework reformed the cheap food industry by stressing pace, proficiency, and consistency in food readiness and administration.

   The Speedee Administration Framework presented an improved on menu, a kitchen mechanical production system, and an emphasis on conveying orders rapidly. Clients could encounter another degree of proficiency, with their dinners arranged in record time. This approach not just separate McDonald's from customary eat in cafés yet additionally laid the basis for future developments that would upgrade the general client experience.

2. **Presentation of the Drive-In and Carhops:**

While the drive-through idea as far as we might be concerned today was still not too far off, McDonald's made a stride towards improving comfort with the presentation of drive-ins and carhops. During the 1950s, a few McDonald's areas tried different things with drive-in help, permitting clients to submit their requests from their vehicles and have their feasts conveyed via carhops - servers on roller skates.

This development was a forerunner to the drive-through model, exhibiting McDonald's obligation to adjusting its administration organization to meet the developing necessities of a vehicle driven society. The drive-in idea, albeit fleeting, denoted an early investigation of furnishing clients with the choice of remaining in their vehicles for a speedy and helpful feasting experience.

3. **Birth of the Drive-through Idea (1970s):**

The genuine unrest in cheap food administration came during the 1970s with the introduction of the drive-through idea. While drive-in help had been tried previously, it was Beam Kroc, the visionary chief who assumed control over the McDonald's establishment framework, who saw the undiscovered capacity of a more smoothed out and productive drive-through experience.

The primary authority McDonald's drive-through opened in Sierra Vista, Arizona, in 1975. The drive-through idea permitted clients to submit their requests through a speaker framework, drive to an assigned window to pay and get their food, all without leaving the solace of their vehicles. This development not just changed the manner in which individuals got to cheap food yet additionally turned into an image of speed and comfort.

The outcome of the drive-through idea was additionally energized by cultural changes, including the ascent of double pay families and the rising speed of current life. The drive-through offered a fast answer for occupied people and families, adjusting impeccably with the in a hurry way of life that was turning out to be more pervasive.

4. **Execution of Computerized Innovations:**

In the 21st hundred years, McDonald's has kept on pushing the limits of administration development by utilizing computerized advancements to upgrade the client experience. The execution of self-request stands, portable requesting applications, and computerized installment choices has changed the customary requesting process, giving clients more control and customization.

Self-request booths, presented in different McDonald's areas all around the world, permit clients to peruse the menu, redo their orders, and complete exchanges freely. This speeds up the requesting system as well as diminishes the probability of mistakes, as clients can include their inclinations straightforwardly into the framework.

Portable requesting applications have turned into a foundation of McDonald's computerized methodology, empowering clients to put in and pay for their requests utilizing their cell phones. This degree of comfort resounds with an educated buyer base that values effectiveness and consistent exchanges.

Besides, McDonald's has embraced the utilization of computerized innovation in the drive-through itself. Double point administration, where orders are taken at two unique places in the drive-through path, and computerized menu loads up that can progressively change in light of elements like climate or season of day, exhibit the brand's obligation to utilizing information and innovation for an improved client experience.

5. **24-Hour Administration and The entire Day Breakfast:**
Perceiving the changing examples of purchaser conduct and the longing for adaptability, McDonald's has executed imaginative help models, for example, 24-hour activities and the presentation of the entire day breakfast. These drives take care of a different client base with fluctuating timetables and inclinations.

The expansion to 24-hour administration at many McDonald's areas worldwide mirrors a promise to openness. Clients can fulfill their McDonald's desires whenever of the day or night, lining up with the requests of a day in and day out way of life and giving an option in contrast to conventional eating limitations.

The presentation of the entire day breakfast was a reaction to buyer interest for greater adaptability in menu decisions. By offering breakfast things over the course of the day, McDonald's addressed the necessities of clients who appreciate breakfast choices at modern hours. This move widened the allure of the menu as well as displayed McDonald's readiness in adjusting to advancing shopper assumptions.

6. **Contactless Assistance During the Coronavirus Pandemic:**
The worldwide Coronavirus pandemic introduced phenomenal difficulties to the café business, requiring quick transformations to guarantee the wellbeing of clients and representatives. McDonald's answered by executing contactless assistance measures, accentuating drive-through, conveyance, and curbside pickup choices.

Drive-through help, currently a foundation of McDonald's tasks, acquired significantly more prominent unmistakable quality during the pandemic. Improved security conventions, including contactless installment choices and limited actual contact, exhibited McDonald's obligation to focusing on the prosperity of the two clients and staff.

The pandemic additionally sped up the execution of advances to work with contactless exchanges and limit face to face collaborations. Versatile requesting, computerized installment, and request ahead highlights became essential parts of the McDonald's administration model, guaranteeing that clients could partake in their number one dinners with upgraded security estimates set up.

7. **Maintainable Assistance Practices:**

Notwithstanding developments in comfort and availability, McDonald's has progressively centered around supportable assistance rehearses. Drives pointed toward decreasing waste, upgrading energy utilization, and embracing eco-accommodating bundling mirror a pledge to natural obligation.

The execution of energy-productive advances in café tasks, like Drove lighting and energy the board frameworks, lines up with McDonald's more extensive manageability objectives. The organization's obligation to involving sustainable power and accomplishing carbon nonpartisanship in its tasks highlights a devotion to limiting its natural impression.

Moreover, McDonald's has made progress in supportable bundling, with a promise to source 100 percent of visitor bundling from sustainable, reused, or confirmed sources by 2025. These drives feature an all encompassing way to deal with administration development that thinks about client comfort as well as the more extensive effect on the climate.

8. **Local area Driven Assistance Drives:**

McDonald's has reliably perceived the significance of local area commitment and administration drives past the walls of its cafés. The foundation of the Ronald McDonald House Noble cause (RMHC) in 1974 is a demonstration of McDonald's obligation to supporting families during testing times, giving lodging and assets to families with debilitated youngsters getting clinical treatment.

Local area driven help reaches out to nearby sponsorships, instructive projects, and associations with altruistic associations. These drives go past the conditional parts of administration, underlining McDonald's job as a corporate resident that contributes emphatically to the networks it serves.

Drive-through and Then some - A Tradition of Administration Development:

Mcdonald's, with its rich history spreading over many years, has become interchangeable with inexpensive food as well as with a tradition of administration development. From the beginning of the Speedee Administration Framework to the weighty presentation of the drive-through idea, McDonald's has ceaselessly advanced to meet the changing requirements and assumptions for its assorted client base.

The drive-through, specifically, stands apart as a progressive idea that has formed the whole cheap food industry. It addresses something other than a helpful method for requesting food; it typifies the soul of development and versatility that characterizes McDonald's as a worldwide forerunner in the fast assistance eatery area.

As McDonald's keeps on embracing computerized innovations, manageability drives, and local area driven help, the brand supports its obligation to giving extraordinary tasting food as well as a client experience that rises above the conventional limits of cheap food. The tradition of administration development at McDonald's is a demonstration of its capacity to remain on the ball, guaranteeing that the Brilliant Curves stay a reference point of comfort, openness, and client driven help in the consistently advancing scene of the cheap food industry.

6.3 McDonald's role in shaping consumer expectations and trends

"Brilliant Curves and Evolving Tastes: McDonald's Part in Molding Buyer Assumptions and Patterns"

Mcdonald's, with its obvious Brilliant Curves, plays had a focal impact in molding the cheap food industry as well as customer assumptions and patterns on a worldwide scale. From acquainting imaginative menu things with spearheading administration ideas, McDonald's has been an innovator, impacting what we eat as well as how we eat. This account investigates the multi-layered effect of McDonald's on buyer culture, analyzing the manners by which the brand has molded preferences, affected eating propensities, and answered advancing cultural assumptions.

1. **The Introduction of Inexpensive Food Culture:**

   McDonald's development during the twentieth century matched with a change in cultural elements, set apart by expanded urbanization, changing work designs, and the ascent of an all the more high speed way of life. The Speedee Administration Framework, spearheaded by the McDonald siblings during the 1940s, established the groundwork for what might turn into the cheap food culture. The smoothed out course of requesting, getting ready, and serving food immediately resounded with a general public looking for proficiency and comfort.

   As McDonald's extended under the authority of Beam Kroc, the idea of inexpensive food became inseparable from the brand. The famous Brilliant Curves turned into an image of a spot to eat as well as of a better approach for feasting — one that was speedy, open, and reasonable. McDonald's assumed a vital part in molding the social shift towards in a hurry eating, impacting purchaser assumptions for speed and comfort.

2. **Normalization and Consistency:**

   One of McDonald's vital commitments to customer assumptions in the cheap food industry is the accentuation on normalization and consistency. The McDonald's model, with its emphasis on consistency in menu things, planning strategies, and administration conveyance, set a benchmark for quality control in the business.

   The execution of severe functional principles guaranteed that a Major Macintosh in one area tasted equivalent to a Major Macintosh in another, paying little mind to geological area. This obligation to consistency added to McDonald's worldwide accomplishment as well as laid out a point of reference for cheap food chains around the world. Shoppers generally expected a normalized experience when they entered any McDonald's café, supporting the thought that cheap food ought to be dependably steady.

3. **Advancement in Menu Contributions:**

   McDonald's has been at the front of menu advancement, presenting things that poor person just become famous however have additionally impacted more extensive culinary patterns. The Filet-O-Fish, Chicken McNuggets, and the Egg McMuffin are only a couple of instances of McDonald's menu things that lastingly affect purchaser tastes.

The progress of these developments has impacted not exclusively McDonald's rivals yet additionally the more extensive food industry. The presentation of the McFlurry, for example, flagged a shift towards more liberal and adjustable sweet choices in the cheap food scene. McDonald's capacity to check and answer changing customer inclinations has started precedents and made a far reaching influence across the business.

4. **The Appearance of the Drive-through:**

The presentation of the drive-through idea by McDonald's during the 1970s not just reformed the manner in which individuals got to cheap food yet in addition set another norm for comfort in the business. The drive-through became inseparable from the McDonald's insight, offering clients a quicker and more open method for partaking in their number one feasts.

This advancement formed shopper assumptions around speed as well as affected the plan and functional procedures of cheap food chains worldwide. The drive-through, when thought about a curiosity, turned into a staple element for speedy help eateries, mirroring a more extensive change in purchaser inclinations towards in a hurry feasting.

5. **Globalization and Social Confinement:**

McDonald's worldwide development carried with it a special test - how to interest different preferences and social inclinations. Accordingly, McDonald's spearheaded the idea of social restriction, adjusting its menu to suit the culinary inclinations of various locales.

In India, where meat isn't broadly consumed, McDonald's presented veggie lover choices like the McAloo Tikki. In Japan, things like the Teriyaki Burger take care of neighborhood flavor profiles. The capacity to offset worldwide consistency with neighborhood customization set a norm for global cheap food chains and exhibited's comprehension McDonald might interpret the significance of social subtleties in molding customer decisions.

6. **Advertising and Marking Impact:**

McDonald's has been a stunning player in the realm of showcasing, forming buyer discernments and impacting buying choices. The brand's notable publicizing efforts, from the "I'm Lovin' It" jingle to the noteworthy characters like Ronald McDonald, have become imbued in mainstream society.

The impact of McDonald's showcasing reaches out past individual items to the more extensive idea of cheap food. The brand's relationship with bliss, accommodation, and reasonableness has added to the standardization of cheap food in day to day existence. McDonald's showcasing techniques have molded purchaser assumptions as well as impacted how society perspectives and values inexpensive food as a social peculiarity.

7. **Innovation and Computerized Commitment:**

In the computerized age, McDonald's has embraced innovation to upgrade client commitment and smooth out the requesting system. The execution of self-request booths, portable applications, and computerized installment choices mirrors a promise to measuring up to the assumptions of educated shoppers.

McDonald's computerized drives furnish accommodation as well as line up with changing buyer ways of behaving. The "Make Your Taste" stage, permitting clients to tweak their burgers, and the combination of versatile requesting and conveyance administrations take special care of a craving for personalization and on-request comfort. These mechanical headways have set a norm for the joining of computerized arrangements in the cheap food industry.

8. **Social Obligation and Wellbeing Awareness:**

As cultural mentalities towards wellbeing and wellbeing have developed, McDonald's has answered by integrating better choices into its menu and showing a promise to social obligation. The incorporation of servings of mixed greens, the expulsion of fake additives, and the presentation of dietary data on menus mirror a more extensive pattern towards wellbeing cognizant feasting.

McDonald's commitment to social obligation drives, like the foundation of the Ronald McDonald House Good cause and responsibilities to economical obtaining, impacts shopper impression of the brand. This attention on moral and socially dependable practices lines up with changing buyer values and assumptions for organizations to contribute decidedly to society.

9. **Adjusting to Evolving Socioeconomics:**

McDonald's has shown a capacity to adjust to changing socioeconomics and cultural movements. The presentation of the entire day breakfast, for instance, answers the inclinations of a different customer base with changing timetables. This adaptability in menu contributions lines up with the assumptions for a cutting edge, dynamic culture that values decision and customization.

Moreover, McDonald's has put forth attempts to take care of the inclinations of more youthful ages by integrating patterns, for example, plant-based choices and supportable practices. This flexibility mirrors a comprehension of the significance of remaining applicable to advancing buyer socioeconomics.

10. **Impacting Culinary Patterns Past Cheap Food:**

The effect of McDonald's reaches out past its own menu and administration model, affecting more extensive culinary patterns. The progress of cheap food as an idea, spearheaded by Mcdonald's, has added to the ascent of fast help eating across the eatery business. The idea of speed, comfort, and moderateness in food administration has become imbued in current customer assumptions, molding the scene of eating foundations universally.

Chapter 7

Global Expansion

"Brilliant Curves Across Boundaries: McDonald's Worldwide Development Excursion"

The story of McDonald's isn't bound to its American roots; it's a story of worldwide reach and the foundation of the Brilliant Curves as a notable image traversing landmasses. The excursion of McDonald's from a little drive-through joint in San Bernardino, California, to a worldwide force to be reckoned with a presence in essentially every edge of the world is a demonstration of the brand's capacity to adjust, enhance, and explore different societies. This investigation dives into the complexities of McDonald's worldwide extension, looking at the key achievements, difficulties, and systems that have molded the brand's global impression.

1. **Early Global Raids:**
   McDonald's left on its worldwide excursion somewhat right off the bat in its set of experiences, perceiving the potential for worldwide development. The principal McDonald's café outside the US opened in Canada in 1967, denoting the underlying strides towards turning into a genuinely global brand. This move was trailed by the foundation of McDonald's areas in nations like Puerto Rico and Costa Rica.

   The outcome of these early endeavors laid the preparation for more aggressive global development plans. Beam Kroc, the main impetus behind McDonald's worldwide vision, was instrumental in planning techniques to adjust the brand to various social settings while keeping up with the center standards of effectiveness and consistency that characterized the McDonald's insight.

2. **The European Development:**
   During the 1970s, McDonald's focused on Europe, a landmass with different culinary practices and customer inclinations. The main European McDonald's opened in the Netherlands in 1971, trailed by areas in Germany and France. The

venture into Europe introduced the two amazing open doors and difficulties as McDonald's explored social subtleties and neighborhood tastes.

One of the key techniques utilized during the European development was the variation of menus to suit neighborhood inclinations. For example, in India, where meat utilization is restricted, McDonald's presented a scope of vegan choices. This adaptability in menu contributions turned into a sign of McDonald's worldwide procedure, displaying a readiness to fit the eating experience to different business sectors.

3. **The Asian Boondocks:**

The 1980s denoted McDonald's entrance into the Asian market, a district known for its rich culinary variety. The main McDonald's in Asia opened in Tokyo, Japan, in 1971. The Asian development introduced novel difficulties as McDonald's experienced social subtleties, different dietary patterns, and a fluctuated scene of neighborhood cooking styles.

In Japan, McDonald's embraced a confinement procedure, presenting things like the Teriyaki Burger to take special care of Japanese taste inclinations. Likewise, in China, McDonald's explored a quickly changing monetary scene and adjusted its way to deal with suit the inclinations of Chinese customers. The progress of McDonald's in Asia reflected a worldwide brand's capacity to adjust as well as the mix of Western cheap food into different culinary customs.

4. **Development in Latin America:**

McDonald's proceeded with its worldwide walk by laying out a presence in Latin America during the 1980s and 1990s. Brazil turned into the primary country in the district to invite McDonald's in 1979. The venture into Latin America carried McDonald's into contact with lively societies, various scenes, and a range of culinary impacts.

In nations like Mexico, McDonald's coordinated nearby flavors into its menu, perceiving the significance of resounding with the inclinations of the populace. The brand's outcome in Latin America showed its nimbleness in exploring the subtleties of each market while maintaining the center components that characterized the McDonald's insight.

5. **Difficulties and Contentions:**

While McDonald's worldwide extension was for the most part met with progress, it was not without difficulties and debates. The brand turned into an image of globalization, confronting reactions connected with social colonialism, unfortunate dietary practices, and work issues. In certain nations, McDonald's turned into a point of convergence for hostile to globalization fights, with worries raised about the effect of cheap food on neighborhood diets and economies.

One remarkable illustration of obstruction was the "McDonald's Burger College" in France, where dissenters designated the development of a McDonald's café close to the noteworthy site of the College of Paris. These difficulties featured the fragile equilibrium that worldwide brands should strike while entering new business sectors and exploring social awarenesses.

6. **Neighborhood Transformation and Development:**
McDonald's progress in worldwide development is attached in its capacity to adjust and advance while remaining consistent with its guiding principle. The idea of "glocalization," mixing worldwide and neighborhood impacts, turned into a core value. McDonald's perceived that while consistency in brand and quality was fundamental, customization in light of nearby preferences was similarly pivotal.

The presentation of area explicit menu things, festivity of neighborhood celebrations through limited time missions, and commitment to local area drives were all important for McDonald's system to implant itself in the texture of different social orders. This versatility charmed McDonald's to neighborhood shoppers as well as built up the brand's obligation to being a piece of the networks it served.

7. **Diversifying Model and Joining forces with Local people:**
A vital calculate McDonald's worldwide extension methodology has been its dependence on the establishment model. Diversifying permitted McDonald's proportional quickly by utilizing nearby business people who had a profound comprehension of the market. The franchisees assumed a urgent part in guaranteeing that McDonald's could explore nearby guidelines, inclinations, and social standards really.

The organization with nearby franchisees likewise worked with the joining of native bits of knowledge into dynamic cycles. This cooperative methodology sped up the speed of development as well as added to the progress of McDonald's in different business sectors. The nearby information and pioneering soul of franchisees turned into a main thrust behind McDonald's capacity to globally flourish.

8. **Venture into Developing Business sectors:**
In the late twentieth and mid 21st hundreds of years, McDonald's directed its concentration toward developing business sectors, perceiving the development potential in economies encountering quick turn of events.

China, specifically, turned into a point of convergence for McDonald's development, with the main café opening in Shenzhen in 1990. The development in China reflected monetary open doors as well as the rising worldwide allure of Western cheap food.

McDonald's likewise extended its impression in other developing business sectors, including India, Russia, and portions of Africa. The organization's methodology in these districts included a mix of transformation to neighborhood tastes and a pledge to adding to the financial improvement of the nations. The progress in developing business sectors featured McDonald's flexibility to different financial and social scenes.

9. **Computerized Change and Worldwide Availability:**
As innovation progressed, McDonald's embraced advanced change to upgrade its worldwide tasks. The execution of computerized requesting stands, portable applications, and online conveyance administrations became vital parts of the McDonald's insight. This innovative incorporation smoothed out the client venture as well as exemplified McDonald's obligation to remaining at the very front of worldwide availability patterns.

The reception of innovation shifted across locales, for certain business sectors driving in portable installment reconciliation and others zeroing in on developments in conveyance administrations. The worldwide network worked with by computerized stages has permitted McDonald's to make a consistent encounter for clients while adjusting to the different innovative scenes of various nations.

10. **Progressing Advancement and Difficulties:**

Notwithstanding its boundless achievement, McDonald's keeps on confronting difficulties and develop because of changing shopper inclinations, cultural assumptions, and worldwide monetary movements. The ascent of wellbeing cognizant feasting, manageability concerns, and expanded rivalry have incited McDonald's to reevaluate its menu contributions, fixing obtaining, and in general brand picture.

As of late, McDonald's has committed to maintainability, including drives to decrease bundling waste and source fixings dependably. These endeavors mirror an attention to the need to line up with advancing buyer values and address natural worries.

The Brilliant Curves' Worldwide Heritage:
McDonald's worldwide development is an account of versatility, flexibility, and a brand's excursion to turn into a social symbol around the world. From the early introductions to Canada and Europe to exploring the intricacies of Asia, Latin America, and developing business sectors, McDonald's has made a permanent imprint on the worldwide inexpensive food scene.

The outcome of McDonald's across borders isn't just about trading a normalized item yet about drawing in with nearby societies, adjusting to different preferences, and fashioning organizations with business visionaries around the world. The Brilliant Curves have turned into an image of commonality and consistency, rising above geological limits and turning into a piece of the social texture in endless nations.

As McDonald's keeps on exploring the intricacies of the worldwide commercial center, the brand's heritage lies in its capacity to serve billions as well as in its obligation to being a mindful worldwide resident. The continuous development of McDonald's mirrors an acknowledgment of the interconnectedness of our reality and the need to offset worldwide brand consistency with nearby variation. The Brilliant Curves stand tall, as an image of inexpensive food, yet as a getting through insignia of globalization and the common encounters that rise above borders."

7.1 McDonald's expansion into international markets
"Brilliant Curves Across Boundaries: McDonald's Extending Worldwide Impression"

The tale of McDonald's isn't restricted to its American starting points; it's a story of worldwide extension, with the notable Brilliant Curves turning into an image perceived across landmasses. From its modest starting points in San Bernardino, California, McDonald's has developed into a worldwide behemoth, serving billions of clients in different societies. This investigation digs into the intricacies of McDonald's venture into worldwide business sectors, looking at the crucial minutes, difficulties, and techniques that have characterized the brand's worldwide excursion.

1. **Early Worldwide Endeavors:**
   McDonald's initial introduction to worldwide business sectors was set apart by an essential vision to bring the inexpensive food experience past American lines. The primary worldwide McDonald's opened in Canada in 1967, with the organization's administration perceiving the potential for worldwide extension. This underlying step set up for a progression of global endeavors, remembering areas for nations like Puerto Rico and Costa Rica.

   The progress of these early endeavors displayed McDonald's flexibility to various business sectors. The establishment laid during these underlying global extensions underscored the requirement for adaptability in approach, as the brand experienced different shopper inclinations and social scenes.

2. **European Extension and Variation:**
   During the 1970s, McDonald's focused on Europe, a mainland wealthy in culinary customs and different preferences. The primary European McDonald's opened in the Netherlands in 1971, denoting the start of a huge section in the brand's worldwide development. Nonetheless, the European market introduced extraordinary difficulties as McDonald's explored social subtleties and nearby inclinations.

   Variation turned into a vital methodology for progress in Europe. McDonald's presented limited menu things, perceiving the significance of taking special care of local preferences. In France, for example, where culinary customs are exceptionally respected, McDonald's embraced a system of coordinating nearby fixings and flavors into its menu. This approach mirrored a pledge to regarding and lining up with the different culinary societies of the European landmass.

3. **Challenges in Social Awareness:**
   While McDonald's worldwide extension was met with progress in numerous areas, it likewise confronted difficulties established in social responsiveness. The brand turned into an image of globalization, drawing analysis for purportedly homogenizing different culinary scenes and disintegrating nearby food customs. In certain examples, McDonald's turned into an objective for hostile to globalization fights, with worries raised about the effect of cheap food on

neighborhood diets and economies.

One eminent illustration of opposition happened in France, where the development of a McDonald's close to the memorable site of the College of Paris started fights. Pundits considered the presence of McDonald's to be a danger to neighborhood culture, and the episode featured the significance of exploring social responsive qualities and addressing concerns connected with social government.

4. **Asian Extension and Restriction:**

The 1980s saw McDonald's extending its presence into Asia, a locale described by a rich embroidery of culinary customs. The principal McDonald's in Asia opened in Tokyo, Japan, in 1971, denoting the start of an excursion into different Asian business sectors. The Asian extension introduced the two difficulties and open doors as McDonald's experienced different dietary patterns, social subtleties, and tastes.

In Japan, McDonald's embraced a restriction technique, presenting menu things like the Teriyaki Burger to take special care of Japanese inclinations. The outcome in Japan exemplified McDonald's capacity to adjust to nearby societies while keeping up with the center components of its image. This confinement system turned into a diagram for the brand's venture into other Asian business sectors, exhibiting a comprehension of the significance of regarding and embracing territorial variety.

5. **Latin American Presence and Culinary Combination:**

McDonald's proceeded with its worldwide walk with a huge presence in Latin America during the 1980s and 1990s. The brand's venture into nations like Brazil and Mexico carried it into contact with dynamic societies and a range of culinary impacts. In Latin America, McDonald's confronted the test of coordinating its contributions into a district with major areas of strength for a personality.

The Latin American experience featured McDonald's capacity to take part in culinary combination, mixing neighborhood flavors with the brand's worldwide menu. In Brazil, for instance, where nearby inclinations for hamburger are solid, McDonald's presented menu things that consolidated customary Brazilian fixings. This approach not just added to the brand's progress in Latin America yet additionally exhibited a guarantee to regarding and celebrating provincial culinary variety.

6. **Diversifying as a Worldwide Development Model:**

An essential part of McDonald's worldwide extension system has been its dependence on the establishment model. Diversifying permitted McDonald's proportional quickly by utilizing neighborhood business visionaries who had a profound comprehension of the market. The franchisees assumed a significant part in exploring neighborhood guidelines, inclinations, and social standards really.

The establishment model likewise worked with a cooperative methodology, as neighborhood franchisees became accomplices in the brand's prosperity. This technique sped up the speed of extension as well as added to McDonald's capacity to flourish in different business sectors. The neighborhood information and pioneering soul of franchisees turned into a main thrust behind McDonald's worldwide development.

7. **Computerized Change for Worldwide Availability:**
As the world entered the computerized age, McDonald's embraced innovation to upgrade its worldwide activities. The execution of advanced requesting booths, versatile applications, and online conveyance administrations became vital parts of the McDonald's insight. This mechanical mix smoothed out the client venture as well as exemplified McDonald's obligation to remaining at the front of worldwide network patterns.

The reception of innovation changed across districts, for certain business sectors driving in versatile installment joining and others zeroing in on developments in conveyance administrations. The worldwide network worked with by computerized stages permitted McDonald's to make a consistent encounter for clients while adjusting to the assorted innovative scenes of various nations.

8. **Developing Business sectors and Financial Open doors:**
In the late twentieth and mid 21st hundreds of years, McDonald's directed its concentration toward developing business sectors, perceiving the development potential in economies encountering quick turn of events. China arose as a point of convergence for McDonald's development, with the primary eatery opening in Shenzhen in 1990. The venture into developing business sectors featured monetary open doors as well as the rising worldwide allure of Western cheap food.

McDonald's likewise extended its impression in other developing business sectors, including India, Russia, and portions of Africa. The organization's methodology in these districts included a mix of variation to neighborhood tastes and a pledge to adding to the monetary improvement of the nations. The outcome in developing business sectors displayed McDonald's versatility to assorted financial and social scenes.

9. **Offsetting Worldwide Consistency with Neighborhood Transformation:**
One of the critical difficulties for McDonald's in worldwide extension has been finding some kind of harmony between worldwide brand consistency and nearby transformation. While keeping up with normalized quality and administration is fundamental for the brand, customization in light of neighborhood tastes and social inclinations is similarly essential for progress.

McDonald's has explored this sensitive equilibrium by presenting district explicit menu things, celebrating neighborhood celebrations through limited time crusades, and taking part in local area drives. This flexibility charmed McDonald's to neighborhood shoppers as well as built up the brand's obligation to being an indispensable piece of the networks it served.

10. Progressing Development and Responsiveness:

Regardless of its far reaching achievement, McDonald's keeps on advancing in light of changing shopper inclinations, cultural assumptions, and worldwide monetary movements. The brand has genuinely committed to maintainability, including drives to lessen bundling waste and source fixings mindfully. These endeavors mirror an attention to the need to line up with developing customer values and address ecological worries.

McDonald's venture into worldwide business sectors is a powerful story of versatility, key development, and a guarantee to turning into a worldwide brand with a neighborhood contact. From exploring social aversions to embracing culinary variety and utilizing innovation for worldwide network, McDonald's process embodies the intricacies and potential open doors innate in growing across borders. The Brilliant Curves have become in excess of an image of cheap food; they address a scaffold between societies, a demonstration of the worldwide interconnectedness of our reality."

7.2 Cultural challenges and adaptations

"Social Difficulties and Variations: McDonald's Worldwide Odyssey"

McDonald's worldwide extension has not been without its reasonable portion of difficulties, large numbers of which come from the unpredictable embroidery of societies that characterize the assorted nations it enters. Exploring social scenes, culinary practices, and cultural standards has been a nonstop excursion for Mcdonald's, requesting a fragile harmony between keeping up with its center character and adjusting to the inclinations and responsive qualities of neighborhood markets. This investigation digs into the social difficulties looked by McDonald's and the versatile systems that have characterized its worldwide odyssey.

1. Culinary Responsiveness and Confinement:

One of the essential difficulties for McDonald's in entering new business sectors has been regarding and adjusting to different culinary practices. Culinary responsiveness goes past only contribution different menu things; it includes figuring out the subtleties of neighborhood flavors, fixings, and dietary patterns. McDonald's initial encounters in nations like Japan and France featured the significance of embracing culinary aversion to acquire acknowledgment in these business sectors.

In Japan, where the culinary scene is well established in conventional flavors and fastidious show, McDonald's embraced a restriction procedure. The presentation of things like the Teriyaki Burger exhibited an eagerness to coordinate neighborhood tastes into the worldwide menu. Additionally, in France, known for its culinary ability, McDonald's stressed quality fixings and integrated French flavors into its contributions. These early illustrations highlighted the meaning of culinary variation as a foundation of McDonald's worldwide achievement.

2. **Adjusting Normalization and Customization:**

Keeping up with normalized processes and guaranteeing a steady client experience are center precepts of McDonald's worldwide achievement. Notwithstanding, accomplishing this while obliging the requirement for customization to suit nearby preferences is a sensitive difficult exercise. Striking the right balance among normalization and customization has been vital for McDonald's in building a generally conspicuous brand without settling on social importance.

The presentation of locale explicit menu things has been a key methodology. For example, in India, where dietary inclinations frequently incline towards vegetarianism, McDonald's offers a scope of vegan choices like the McAloo Tikki. This approach permits McDonald's to stick to worldwide principles while taking special care of the exceptional preferences and dietary propensities for each market, supporting the brand's versatility.

3. **Social Awareness and Neighborhood Values:**

Past the domain of food, McDonald's has needed to explore different social qualities and cultural standards. Social responsiveness reaches out to understanding and regarding nearby traditions, customs, and social practices. In certain occasions, McDonald's has confronted difficulties when its worldwide picture conflicted with profoundly imbued neighborhood values.

For instance, in dominatingly Hindu India, where the cow is worshipped, McDonald's presented a menu without meat, zeroing in on chicken, fish, and vegan choices. This social transformation mirrored a comprehension of the significance of lining up with neighborhood values and opinions. Likewise, in Islamic nations, McDonald's sticks to Halal guidelines, exhibiting a guarantee to regarding strict and social inclinations.

4. **Brand Discernment and Nearby Personalities:**

Laying out a positive brand discernment in different social settings requires something other than offering natural menu things. McDonald's has needed to explore the impression of its image corresponding to neighborhood personalities cautiously. In certain examples, the Brilliant Curves have been viewed as images of Westernization, provoking opposition and against globalization feelings.

In France, especially, where culinary customs are well established, McDonald's confronted resistance that went past culinary worries. Pundits saw McDonald's as a danger to neighborhood personality and an image of American social government. Accordingly, McDonald's taken on techniques to underscore its obligation to nearby networks, including drives like obtaining fixings locally and participating in local area improvement projects.

5. **Language and Correspondence Difficulties:**

Viable correspondence is fundamental for any worldwide brand, and McDonald's is no exemption. Language contrasts present a special arrangement of difficulties, from menu interpretations to publicizing efforts. McDonald's has perceived the significance of clear and socially fitting correspondence in building associations with nearby buyers.

In multilingual nations like Canada, McDonald's guarantees that its menu and publicizing materials are accessible in both English and French, regarding the etymological variety of the populace. Past etymological contemplations, McDonald's has likewise customized its promoting messages to resound with social subtleties, embracing nearby VIPs and social references to upgrade appeal.

6. **Local area Commitment and Nearby Organizations:**
Social variation goes past menu things and showcasing methodologies; it stretches out to local area commitment and building significant associations. McDonald's progress in different business sectors has been dependent upon its capacity to coordinate into the texture of neighborhood networks, exhibiting a pledge to social obligation and social appreciation.

In India, McDonald's has participated in local area driven drives, supporting neighborhood causes and praising celebrations through exceptional advancements. Essentially, in Latin America, McDonald's has supported nearby occasions and embraced local area contribution. These endeavors go past deals, cultivating a feeling of having a place and acknowledgment inside nearby networks.

7. **Administrative Consistence and Neighborhood Regulations:**
Complying with nearby guidelines and legitimate systems is a basic part of McDonald's worldwide tasks. Various nations have assorted guidelines overseeing food handling, work practices, and business tasks. McDonald's has needed to explore these guidelines, guaranteeing consistence while maintaining its worldwide norms.

For example, in a few European nations, there are severe guidelines connected with the obtaining of fixings and promoting to youngsters. McDonald's has changed its practices to line up with these guidelines, exhibiting a readiness to adjust its plan of action to the legitimate systems of each market. This flexibility is significant for legitimate consistence as well as for building entrust with nearby specialists and purchasers.

8. **Moral Obtaining and Ecological Contemplations:**
As worldwide attention to moral obtaining and natural maintainability has risen, McDonald's has confronted difficulties connected with adjusting its practices to developing shopper values. Social transformation, in this specific circumstance, includes understanding neighborhood assumptions as well as proactively addressing concerns connected with dependable strategic policies.

In light of ecological worries, McDonald's has swore to decrease its natural impression by carrying out feasible obtaining practices and diminishing bundling waste. This responsibility mirrors a comprehension of the rising significance of natural cognizance in different societies and lines up with the brand's endeavors to be a capable corporate resident.

9. **Emergency The executives and Notoriety Insurance:**
Social difficulties at times manifest as emergencies that compromise a brand's standing. McDonald's has experienced circumstances where negative episodes, whether connected with food handling or social heartlessness, can possibly harm its picture. Compelling emergency the board includes settling prompt issues as well as remaking trust and adjusting methodologies to forestall comparative occurrences.

In occasions where sanitation concerns emerged, McDonald's executed measures to address and forestall such issues, exhibiting a pledge to shopper prosperity. Moreover, McDonald's has put resources into social responsiveness preparing for its staff to keep away from episodes that could be seen as rude or hostile in different business sectors.

10. **Persistent Learning and Variation:**

Maybe the most essential part of social variation for McDonald's has been the acknowledgment that it is a continuous interaction. The worldwide scene is dynamic, with social inclinations, cultural standards, and customer assumptions developing constantly. McDonald's progress in worldwide business sectors is, generally, ascribed to its capacity to gain from encounters, adjust procedures, and remain sensitive to social movements.

The foundation of restricted development communities and examination offices mirrors McDonald's obligation to remaining in front of social patterns. By constantly assembling bits of knowledge and input from neighborhood advertises, McDonald's can proactively change its menu, promoting, and functional techniques to remain socially important.

Social Variation as an Essential Goal:
McDonald's worldwide excursion is a demonstration of the brand's capacity to explore the unpredictable difficulties presented by different societies. Social transformation has been vital to McDonald's prosperity, molding not exclusively its menu contributions and showcasing methodologies yet in addition its way of life as a dependable worldwide resident. The brand's obligation to understanding, regarding, and embracing social variety has permitted it to rise above being simply a cheap food chain and turned into an image of interconnectedness in a globalized world.

As McDonald's proceeds with its worldwide odyssey, the examples gained from social difficulties and variations will stay significant. The capacity to offset worldwide consistency with nearby pertinence, embrace variety, and contribute emphatically to the networks it serves characterizes McDonald's continuous story. The Brilliant Curves, with their worldwide engraving, stand as images of inexpensive food as well as reference points of social versatility and a common worldwide encounter."

7.3 The emergence of McDonald's as a global brand

"The Rise of McDonald's as a Worldwide Brand: From Brilliant Curves to Worldwide Symbol"

McDonald's striking process from a little drive-through eatery in San Bernardino, California, to a worldwide peculiarity with a pervasive presence on pretty much every landmass is a demonstration of the brand's strength, development, and flexibility. The development of McDonald's as a worldwide brand is a complex story that entwines components of business, vital vision, and social reverberation. This investigation dives into the vital elements and extraordinary minutes that impelled McDonald's into a worldwide symbol.

1. **Beam Kroc's Vision and Enterprising Drive:**
   The narrative of McDonald's as a worldwide brand is unpredictably attached to the vision and innovative soul of Beam Kroc, a man who might become inseparable from the Brilliant Curves. During the 1950s, Kroc, a milkshake machine sales rep, coincidentally found Richard and Maurice McDonald's little yet progressive San Bernardino café. The siblings had spearheaded an arrangement of cheap food creation that stressed speed, consistency, and moderateness.
   Perceiving the capability of their creative model, Kroc saw past the humble starting points of the first McDonald's and imagined an organization of normalized eateries serving a reliable menu. In 1955, Kroc established McDonald's Organization, laying the preparation for the brand's change into a worldwide monster.

2. **Normalization and the Introduction of the Establishment Model:**
   Key to McDonald's worldwide achievement was the idea of normalization. Kroc understood that to scale the business, it was vital to keep up with consistency in both the item and the client experience. This prompted the improvement of an extensive tasks manual, illustrating all that from cooking techniques to the plan of the eateries.
   The presentation of the establishment model turned into the key part of McDonald's development technique. Diversifying permitted the brand to quickly recreate its effective model with the assistance of neighborhood business visionaries who shared a personal stake in the progress of their singular cafés. This decentralized way to deal with proprietorship worked with the brand's entrance into different business sectors and guaranteed neighborhood transformation.

3. **The Brilliant Curves and Brand Personality:**
   The notorious Brilliant Curves, planned by draftsman Stanley Meston during the 1950s, turned into an image inseparable from Mcdonald's. The unmistakable curves, initially an actual component of the eatery engineering, developed into a strong brand character. The Brilliant Curves, with their striking, unmistakable plan, came to address something other than a spot to snatch a speedy dinner; they represented a worldwide brand offering commonality and consistency.
   The essential utilization of the Brilliant Curves in marking and promoting efforts built up the visual character of Mcdonald's. Whether in the clamoring

roads of New York City or on the tranquil streets of a rustic town, the Brilliant Curves turned into a general image, rising above semantic and social hindrances.

4. **Showcasing Developments and the Blissful Dinner Peculiarity:**

McDonald's prosperity as a worldwide brand is likewise credited to showcasing developments reverberated with different crowds. The presentation of the Cheerful Feast in 1979, highlighting a little toy with a kid's dinner, turned into a social peculiarity. This showcasing technique spoke to youngsters as well as made a vital and positive relationship with the brand for families all over the planet.

Additionally, McDonald's embraced provincial showcasing efforts that recognized neighborhood customs and merriments. By interfacing with purchasers on a social level, McDonald's built up its obligation to being a piece of the networks it served, further hardening its worldwide allure.

5. **Advancement in Menu Contributions:**

While keeping a center menu of internationally perceived things like the Huge Macintosh and Chicken McNuggets, McDonald's additionally displayed an eagerness to adjust its menu to neighborhood tastes. The idea of "glocalization," mixing worldwide and nearby impacts, permitted McDonald's to present district explicit things that reverberated with different palates.

For example, in India, where most of the populace follows veggie lover dietary inclinations, McDonald's presented the McAloo Tikki, a vegan burger custom fitted to nearby preferences. This approach exhibited a comprehension of the significance of offering menu decisions that line up with social inclinations, a system that added to McDonald's acknowledgment in different worldwide business sectors.

6. **Embracing Innovation and Comfort:**

McDonald's obligation to advancement reached out to embracing innovation to improve client accommodation. The presentation of drive-through administrations reformed the cheap food experience, giving a speedy and proficient way for clients to arrange and accept their feasts without leaving their vehicles. This variation to changing shopper ways of behaving exemplified McDonald's responsiveness to advancing ways of life.

Lately, McDonald's has kept on utilizing innovation with the execution of self-administration booths, versatile requesting, and conveyance administrations. These innovative headways not just take special care of the inclinations of a well informed purchaser base yet in addition exhibit McDonald's obligation to remaining at the front line of industry patterns.

7. **Social Versatility and Local area Incorporation:**

McDonald's prosperity as a worldwide brand can be credited to its capacity to adjust to different societies while keeping a reliable brand picture. The brand's way to deal with social versatility includes something beyond menu customization; it reaches out to local area commitment and incorporation.

In various nations, McDonald's has embraced nearby practices and far-reaching developments, adjusting its showcasing efforts with local celebrations. By effectively taking part in neighborhood networks, McDonald's has situated itself as a cheap food chain as well as a piece of the social texture, adding to its acknowledgment and accomplishment all over the planet.

8. **Difficulties and Discussions:**

The rise of McDonald's as a worldwide brand has not been without difficulties and contentions. The brand turned into a lightning bar for analysis connected with issues, for example, undesirable dietary patterns, natural effect, and work rehearses. McDonald's answered these difficulties with a blend of vital changes and proactive measures.

Drives to give better menu choices, responsibilities to feasible obtaining, and endeavors to address concerns connected with work rehearses displayed McDonald's readiness to advance and answer cultural assumptions. The capacity to explore these difficulties built up McDonald's versatility and flexibility on the worldwide stage.

9. **Corporate Social Obligation and Maintainability:**

As McDonald's developed into a worldwide brand, the idea of corporate social obligation (CSR) became basic to its character. McDonald's perceived the significance of rewarding the networks it served and started different CSR programs. This obligation to social obligation went past generosity; it turned into an essential basic for building a positive brand picture.

Lately, McDonald's has made progress in manageability by vowing to capably source its food and bundling. These drives line up with developing buyer mindfulness and assumptions about moral strategic policies, exhibiting McDonald's commitment to being a dependable worldwide resident.

10. **The Brilliant Curves Across Landmasses:**

Today, McDonald's stands as a worldwide brand with a presence in more than 100 nations, serving a large number of clients day to day. The Brilliant Curves have turned into a getting through image of cheap food as well as of worldwide network and shared encounters. Whether in the core of clamoring metropolitan focuses or in distant country scenes, McDonald's is an unmistakable installation, a demonstration of its effective rise as a worldwide brand.

The development of McDonald's as a worldwide brand is a story molded by development, flexibility, and a promise to understanding and embracing different societies. From the vision of Beam Kroc to the famous Brilliant Curves, McDonald's process reflects not just the development of an inexpensive food chain yet additionally the change of a brand into a worldwide social peculiarity. As McDonald's proceeds to develop and confront new difficulties, its persevering through worldwide heritage is scratched in the shared perspective of buyers all over the planet."

Chapter 8

Legacy and Impact

"Brilliant Curves Heritage and Effect: The Persevering through Impact of McDonald's on Worldwide Culture"

The tradition of Mcdonald's, set apart by the famous Brilliant Curves, stretches out a long ways past its starting points as an unassuming drive-thru eatery in San Bernardino, California. As the brand commends many years of worldwide achievement, its effect on culture, business, and society remains as a demonstration of the groundbreaking force of business, development, and versatility. This investigation dives into the heritage and effect of Mcdonald's, inspecting the persevering through impact that has made a permanent imprint on the texture of worldwide culture.

1. **Forming the Inexpensive Food Industry:**
   McDonald's isn't simply a member in the cheap food industry; it is a spearheading force that has on a very basic level molded the scene of fast help cafés around the world. The establishment model presented by Beam Kroc turned into an outline for development, empowering McDonald's to multiply quickly across different business sectors. The accentuation on normalization, speed, and reasonableness set another norm for proficiency in the business.
   The effect of McDonald's on the cheap food area is clear in the various chains that went with the same pattern, embracing comparative methodologies to accomplish adaptability and consistency. The Brilliant Curves became inseparable from a smoothed out and replicable plan of action, everlastingly modifying the elements of how individuals all over the planet devour food in a hurry.

2. **Normalization versus Restriction:**
   A critical part of McDonald's heritage lies in its capacity to figure out some kind of harmony between worldwide normalization and nearby transformation. The normalized processes, from the planning of food to café configuration, guaranteed a steady brand insight across mainlands. This approach was progressive

with regards to the cheap food industry, where quick help and consistency were not generally focused on.

Notwithstanding, McDonald's likewise perceived the significance of adjusting to nearby preferences and social subtleties. The presentation of district explicit menu things exhibited a readiness to embrace variety and take special care of the inclinations of various business sectors. The pressure among normalization and restriction, explored capably by Mcdonald's, turned into a main trait of world-wide brands looking for acknowledgment in different societies.

3. **Work and Financial Effect:**

McDonald's worldwide impression makes an interpretation of into a tremen-dous organization of eateries as well as into a huge financial effect. The brand's tasks set out business open doors for a huge number of individuals around the world, from cutting edge staff in individual establishments to corporate situ-ations at the central command. The financial impact of McDonald's stretches out to providers, wholesalers, and different subordinate businesses associated with the food and refreshment area.

In numerous networks, especially in developing business sectors, the presence of McDonald's adds to financial development and improvement. The estab-lishment model enables nearby business visionaries to claim and work their organizations, encouraging a feeling of responsibility and business. The finan-cial tradition of Mcdonald's, in this manner, stretches out past the limits of its eateries to impact more extensive monetary environments.

4. **Culinary Globalization and Social Trade:**

McDonald's plays had an essential impact in the peculiarity of culinary global-ization, where food from one culture is embraced and adjusted in different corners of the world. The brand's worldwide menu, highlighting things like the Large Macintosh and Chicken McNuggets, fills in as a social extension, inter-facing individuals with a common culinary encounter.

While certain pundits contend that the spread of worldwide cheap food disinte-grates nearby culinary practices, McDonald's has likewise turned into a material for culinary combination.

Through confined menu things and transformations, McDonald's exhibits a nuanced comprehension of the significance of regarding and coordinating terri-torial flavors. Along these lines, McDonald's has inadvertently turned into a stage for social trade through the widespread language of food.

5. **Purchaser Conduct and Accommodation Culture:**

McDonald's has been a harbinger of a change in customer conduct towards comfort culture. The presentation of drive-through administrations and the accentuation on fast, open feasts added to a change in outlook in how individ-uals see and devour food. The "McDonaldization" of society, a term instituted to depict the impact of cheap food standards on different parts of life, mir-rors the brand's effect on molding shopper assumptions for productivity and promptness.

This development in purchaser conduct, impacted by Mcdonald's, has pervaded past the domain of cheap food. The assumption for comfort and speed has turned into a sign of present day life, influencing businesses going from innovation to retail. Mcdonald's, as a social trailblazer, has played a basic job in forming this more extensive shift towards a comfort situated way of life.

6. **Promoting and Marking Developments:**

The promoting ability of McDonald's has been a main thrust behind its worldwide achievement. The presentation of the Brilliant Curves as a visual character, combined with essential publicizing efforts, made a brand that rose above language obstructions. McDonald's became a spot to eat as well as a social image, profoundly imbued in famous cognizance.

The Cheerful Feast peculiarity, presented in 1979, epitomizes McDonald's creative way to deal with advertising. By partner the brand with youth bliss through little toys included with feasts, McDonald's made an enduring association with more youthful buyers, laying out a client devotion pipeline since the beginning.

7. **Social Obligation and Manageability Drives:**

As cultural assumptions about corporate obligation developed, McDonald's answered with drives pointed toward cultivating a positive effect. The brand's obligation to supportability, moral obtaining, and local area commitment became essential parts of its character. McDonald's perceived that its impact stretched out past the domain of inexpensive food and embraced the obligation of being a worldwide corporate resident.

From endeavors to diminish bundling waste to responsibilities to manageable obtaining of fixings, McDonald's has executed measures to line up with contemporary qualities. The tradition of McDonald's incorporates not exclusively its social effect yet additionally its continuous endeavors to contribute decidedly to ecological and social difficulties.

8. **General Wellbeing and Nourishment Difficulties:**

McDonald's worldwide impact has not been resistant to examination, especially concerning general wellbeing and sustenance. The ascent of worries connected with corpulence and diet-related sicknesses incited a reexamination of cheap food utilization designs. McDonald's answered by presenting better menu choices, giving dietary data, and effectively taking part in discoursed around capable eating.

The general wellbeing tradition of McDonald's is a complicated story that reflects more extensive cultural conversations about the job of cheap food in molding dietary propensities. McDonald's commitment with these conversations, including menu changes and instructive drives, highlights the brand's consciousness of its effect on general wellbeing and its obligation to tending to related difficulties.

9. **Flexibility Notwithstanding Difficulties:**

The persevering through tradition of McDonald's is likewise described by its flexibility despite challenges. From exploring social protection from addressing discussions connected with work rehearses and ecological effect, McDonald's has endured storms that go with worldwide conspicuousness. The brand's capacity to gain from misfortunes, adjust to evolving conditions, and proactively address issues has added to its proceeded with pertinence.

Versatility is implanted in McDonald's DNA, from its initial days as a solitary eatery to its ongoing status as a worldwide monster. The brand's ability to develop and improve in light of difficulties guarantees that it stays a unique power in the steadily changing scene of business and culture.

10. **Social Imagery and Shared Encounters:**

At last, the tradition of McDonald's rises above the domain of business and financial matters to turn into a social image. The Brilliant Curves are not only a logo; they address shared encounters, recollections, and social associations that length ages and topographies. Mcdonald's, through its worldwide reach, has turned into an image of commonality and solace, where individuals from different foundations can settle on some mutual interest.

Whether it's the delight of a Blissful Feast, the smell of newly cooked fries, or the acknowledgment of the Brilliant Curves not too far off, McDonald's has carved itself into the shared mindset of worldwide culture. The brand's getting through heritage lies not just in that frame of mind to serve billions of dinners however in its commitment to the common human experience, making snapshots of association in a world that is progressively interconnected.

Past Inexpensive Food, a Social Peculiarity:

The inheritance and effect of McDonald's reach out a long ways past its job as an inexpensive food goliath. It is an account of business, social trade, and flexibility. From the normalization of inexpensive food cycles to the restriction of menus, from the notable Brilliant Curves to inventive advertising efforts, McDonald's has made a permanent imprint on the worldwide social scene.

As McDonald's keeps on advancing in light of changing buyer assumptions and cultural difficulties, its heritage will keep on unfurling. The Brilliant Curves, with their getting through imagery, will stay not simply a marker of a drive-through joint however a reference point of social network in our current reality where shared encounters are loved and celebrated. The effect of McDonald's on worldwide culture is a story actually being composed, a story that mirrors the steadily developing connection among business and society in the 21st 100 years."

8.1 Kroc's philanthropy and contributions to society

"Beam Kroc's Generosity and Commitments to Society: Past Brilliant Curves"

Beam Kroc, the visionary behind the worldwide progress of Mcdonald's, isn't just associated with changing the inexpensive food industry yet additionally for his humanitarian undertakings and commitments to society. Past the famous Brilliant Curves, Kroc's inheritance is set apart by a guarantee to social obligation, local area commitment, and charity. This investigation dives into the generous excursion of Beam Kroc, featuring the manners by which he looked to have a beneficial outcome on society past the domain of cheap food.

1. **The Early Years and Innovative Soul:**
   Beam Kroc's charitable excursion can be followed back to his initial years and the innovative soul that characterized his profession. Prior to experiencing the McDonald siblings and their creative cheap food model, Kroc was engaged with different undertakings, including selling paper cups and functioning as a Multimixer milkshake machine deals specialist.
   These early encounters imparted in Kroc a feeling of assurance and cleverness. While the attention was at first on building his own undertakings, Kroc's excursion towards magnanimity started to come to fruition as he perceived the more extensive obligations that accompany achievement and flourishing.

2. **The McDonald's Establishment and Schooling Drives:**
   As McDonald's Company developed into a worldwide goliath, Kroc comprehended the significance of rewarding the networks that added to the brand's prosperity. In 1965, he laid out the McDonald's Establishment, a magnanimous association pointed toward supporting schooling drives. The establishment turned into a vehicle for directing assets into programs that helped understudies and instructive foundations.
   Kroc's obligation to instruction stretched out past monetary commitments. He trusted in the groundbreaking force of training to elevate people and networks. Grants, awards, and backing for instructive framework became necessary parts of the McDonald's Establishment's main goal, mirroring Kroc's confidence in giving open doors to people in the future.

3. **Ronald McDonald House Good cause:**
   One of Beam Kroc's most persevering and effective humanitarian inheritances is the foundation of Ronald McDonald House Good cause (RMHC). The thought for RMHC began in 1974 when the Philadelphia Hawks football crew and their Head supervisor, Jim Murray, moved toward Kroc with the vision of supporting groups of genuinely sick youngsters.
   Perceiving the significant effect such a drive might have, Kroc embraced the thought sincerely. The primary Ronald McDonald House opened in Philadelphia in 1974, giving a "usual hangout spot" for families with kids going through clinical treatment. The outcome of this underlying undertaking established the groundwork for the development of RMHC all around the world.
   Today, RMHC works in more than 64 nations and locales, with many Ronald

McDonald Houses, Family Rooms, and Care Mobiles. These offices offer help, housing, and solace to families confronting the difficulties of having a youngster getting clinical consideration. Kroc's vision of RMHC as a foundation of McDonald's charity mirrors a profound obligation to the prosperity of families and networks.

4. **Local area Commitment and Nearby Drives:**
Past the worldwide drives like the McDonald's Establishment and RMHC, Beam Kroc underlined the significance of local area commitment at the nearby level. McDonald's eateries were urged to effectively take part in local area occasions, support nearby games groups, and add to neighborhood advancement projects.

Kroc's way of thinking was established in the conviction that a fruitful business is complicatedly associated with the prosperity of the networks it serves. By cultivating a feeling of local area and adding to neighborhood causes, McDonald's under Kroc's initiative turned out to be something other than a cheap food chain; it turned into a vital piece of the social texture in endless towns and urban communities all over the planet.

5. **Natural Stewardship and Maintainability:**
As natural mindfulness rose in the last option part of the twentieth 100 years, Kroc perceived the significance of integrating maintainability rehearses into McDonald's activities. While this part of Kroc's inheritance is more lined up with corporate obligation than customary generosity, it mirrors a guarantee to limiting the natural effect of the business.

Under Kroc's authority, McDonald's started projects to lessen squander, further develop energy effectiveness, and execute feasible obtaining rehearses. These endeavors, while driven by an acknowledgment of the business basic for natural obligation, likewise added to more extensive conversations about the job of enterprises in tending to ecological difficulties.

6. **Generosity as an Initiative Rule:**
Beam Kroc's way to deal with generosity was not simply a symbolic motion or an advertising methodology. All things considered, it was profoundly imbued in his administration reasoning. Kroc accepted that effective organizations had an ethical constraint to add to the government assistance of society. This rule went past the monetary perspective and remembered dynamic interest for social and local area drives.

Kroc's humanitarian outlook impacted the way of life of McDonald's during his residency as Chief. The possibility that organizations ought to be mindful stewards of their prosperity, effectively captivating with and rewarding the networks that help them, turned into a core value for McDonald's as a worldwide company.

7. **Difficulties and Reactions:**
While Beam Kroc's humanitarian endeavors were significant and effective, they

were not without difficulties and reactions. A few pundits contended that drives like the McDonald's Establishment were lacking to balance the apparent adverse consequences of the inexpensive food industry on wellbeing and the climate. Others scrutinized the inspirations driving magnanimity, seeing it as a type of corporate personal circumstance.

Kroc, in any case, was down to earth about these difficulties. He recognized that generosity couldn't be a panacea for all issues related with the business. In any case, he stayed focused on tending to cultural necessities where conceivable, stressing that capable corporate conduct included a complex methodology that included both generosity and moral strategic policies.

8. **Inheritance Past Corporate Achievement:**

Beam Kroc's inheritance reaches out a long ways past the corporate progress of Mcdonald's. While the Brilliant Curves turned into a universally perceived image of cheap food, Kroc's generous commitments highlighted the more extensive job that organizations can play in forming and improving networks. His conviction that achievement ought to be imparted to society, whether through training drives or supporting families in the midst of hardship, has made a permanent imprint on the corporate world.

The foundation and development of Ronald McDonald House Good cause stand as a demonstration of Kroc's vision of utilizing corporate assets to address significant cultural difficulties. RMHC's effect on the existences of endless families highlights the potential for organizations to be a power for good and contribute emphatically to the networks they serve.

9. **Illustrations for People in the future:**

Beam Kroc's magnanimous excursion offers significant examples for people in the future of business pioneers. It underscores the significance of perceiving the more extensive obligations that accompany corporate achievement. Kroc's way to deal with charity was not value-based however established in a certifiable craving to have a constructive outcome on society.

Business pioneers can gain from Kroc's comprehensive methodology, where altruism is incorporated into the texture of corporate culture and values. The possibility that organizations, no matter what their industry, can contribute genuinely to cultural prosperity is an inheritance that rises above the particulars of cheap food and reverberates across different areas.

10. **An Enduring Effect:**

Beam Kroc died in 1984, yet his effect on charity and corporate obligation keeps on resonating through the tradition of McDonald's and the associations he established. Ronald McDonald House Good cause, specifically, remains as a residing demonstration of Kroc's vision of utilizing corporate assets to address squeezing cultural requirements.

As McDonald's and different companies explore the intricacies of the 21st hundred years, Kroc's heritage fills in as an update that achievement is most significant when imparted to the networks that structure the groundwork of that achievement. The getting through impact of Beam Kroc's charity lies not just in the unmistakable commitments made during his lifetime however in the motivation it accommodates another age of pioneers to think about the more extensive effect of their undertakings on society."

8.2 The lasting impact of McDonald's on the fast-food industry and American culture

"The Enduring Effect of McDonald's on the Cheap Food Industry and American Culture: A Brilliant Heritage"

The account of McDonald's isn't simply a story of cheap food expansion; an account has made a permanent imprint on the inexpensive food industry and American culture at large. From the modest starting points of a little San Bernardino eatery to turning into a worldwide peculiarity, McDonald's has reclassified the manner in which individuals eat food as well as molded the social scene of the US and then some. This investigation dives into the enduring effect of Mcdonald's, inspecting its impact on the inexpensive food industry, shopper conduct, and the social texture of America.

1. **Reforming the Cheap Food Model:**
   The most essential and getting through effect of McDonald's lies in its progressive way to deal with the cheap food model. The advancement presented by Richard and Maurice McDonald during the 1940s, underscoring pace, productivity, and reasonableness, laid the foundation for the change of the whole business. The sequential construction system creation framework, where every laborer had a particular errand, guaranteed predictable and quick help.

   Beam Kroc, perceiving the extraordinary capability of this model, took it higher than ever by diversifying the idea. The establishment model empowered quick extension as well as set a norm for consistency and quality control. This upset cheap food from a confined, mother and-pop undertaking to a versatile, normalized, and internationally replicable plan of action.

2. **Normalization and the Introduction of the Inexpensive Food Culture:**
   McDonald's impact on the inexpensive food industry is inseparable from the idea of normalization. The careful normalization of food readiness processes, cooking times, and, surprisingly, the plan of the cafés turned into the sign of the McDonald's insight. This normalization guaranteed a predictable item as well as made a feeling of commonality for purchasers, no matter what their area.

   The introduction of the inexpensive food culture can be followed back to McDonald's accentuation on speed and accommodation. The possibility that one could get a speedy, reasonable feast without settling on taste or quality turned into a social shift that resounded with the quick moving ways of life of post-war America. McDonald's set the norm for what purchasers generally expected from cheap food foundations, impacting the business as well as more extensive examples of utilization.

3. **Spearheading Promoting and Marking Methodologies:**
McDonald's didn't simply sell cheeseburgers and fries; it sold an encounter, and this was accomplished through spearheading promoting and marking method-ologies. The presentation of the notable Brilliant Curves, planned by draftsman Stanley Meston during the 1950s, turned into a masterstroke in brand person-ality. The Brilliant Curves, with their strong and unmistakable plan, became inseparable from the McDonald's insight.

The promoting advancements stretched out to significant publicizing efforts, snappy mottos, and the production of characters like Ronald McDonald. These methodologies laid out McDonald's as a commonly recognized name as well as added to the brand's social importance. McDonald's wasn't simply a spot to eat; it turned into an image of American industrialism and a social symbol that rose above geological limits.

4. **Forming Shopper Conduct:**
McDonald's assumed a crucial part in forming buyer conduct, presenting the idea of "quick" food and impacting how individuals moved toward feasting out. The speed and proficiency of administration, combined with a menu that zeroed in on fast and effectively consumable things, turned into a layout for the cutting edge cheap food experience. The presentation of drive-through administrations further smoothed out the cycle, making cheap food more helpful than any time in recent memory.

The idea of a normalized menu with notorious things like the Huge Macintosh and Chicken McNuggets became imbued in the shared mindset. McDonald im-pacted individuals ate as well as how they saw eating out. The possibility that a dinner could be speedy, reasonable, and reliable turned into a social assumption that stretched out past the domains of inexpensive food.

5. **Social Imagery and Globalization:**
The Brilliant Curves of McDonald's changed from simple structural elements to strong images of American culture and globalization. As McDonald's extended its scope universally, the Brilliant Curves became inseparable from American impact and social commodity. Seeing those recognizable curves in unfamiliar terrains implied the accessibility of cheap food as well as the impact of American culture on a worldwide scale.

The spread of McDonald's to different nations achieved a peculiarity frequently alluded to as "McDonaldization," where components of American culture, as addressed by Mcdonald's, saturated various social orders. The social effect of McDonald's stretched out past the actual food to incorporate parts of configuration, showcasing, and even client assistance works on, adding to the homogenization of purchaser encounters all over the planet.

6. **Advancing Menu and Culinary Patterns:**
   While McDonald's is frequently connected with a normalized menu, its impact on culinary patterns is more nuanced. The brand's capacity to adjust its menu to neighborhood tastes and inclinations displayed an adaptability that went past the underlying impression of a one-size-fits-all methodology. This idea of "glocalization" permitted McDonald's to present locale explicit things that resounded with different palates.

   Besides, McDonald's assumed a part in promoting specific culinary patterns, presenting things like plates of mixed greens, yogurt parfaits, and better refreshment choices because of changing buyer inclinations. The brand's effect on culinary patterns isn't just about the particular things on its menu yet in addition about the more extensive effect on buyer assumptions for assortment and decision in cheap food contributions.

7. **Business Practices and Industry Guidelines:**
   The effect of McDonald's stretches out to the business practices and industry guidelines inside the cheap food area. The diversifying model presented by Beam Kroc turned into an outline for how inexpensive food chains extended and worked. Diversifying worked with quick development as well as impacted business rehearses by decentralizing possession and putting liability in the possession of neighborhood business visionaries.

   The normalization of cycles, from food readiness to client care, set industry benchmarks. McDonald's turned into a model for proficiency in the cheap food area, and contenders tried to copy its prosperity by taking on comparable functional norms.

   The work rehearses and functional productivity presented by McDonald's have had an enduring effect, forming the standards and assumptions inside the more extensive inexpensive food industry.

8. **General Wellbeing and Cultural Effect:**
   McDonald's has not been safe to investigation in regards to general wellbeing concerns related with cheap food. As the brand became inseparable from accommodation and reasonableness, it additionally confronted analysis connected with issues, for example, weight, unfortunate dietary patterns, and the effect of inexpensive food on general wellbeing. These worries provoked a reconsideration of dietary propensities and set off a more extensive cultural discussion about the job of cheap food in contemporary ways of life.

   McDonald's answered these difficulties by presenting better menu choices, giving dietary data, and effectively captivating openly talk around mindful eating. The brand's readiness to adjust to changing cultural assumptions highlighted its job as a purveyor of food as well as a member in more extensive discussions about general wellbeing and prosperity.

9. **Mechanical Development and Changing Purchaser Propensities:**
   Lately, McDonald's has embraced mechanical development to remain applicable

in a time of changing customer propensities. The presentation of self-adminis-tration stands, portable requesting, and conveyance administrations mirrors the brand's responsiveness to the developing inclinations of a well informed cus-tomer base. Mcdonald's, when an image of quick, face to face administration, has adjusted to the computerized age by integrating innovation into its tasks.

The mechanical developments presented by McDonald's poor person just im-pacted the client experience inside its eateries yet have likewise set a norm for how inexpensive food binds influence innovation to live up to the assumptions of current shoppers. This flexibility to changing shopper propensities highlights McDonald's capacity to stay at the cutting edge of the business notwithstanding advancing patterns.

10. Inheritance and the Brilliant Curves' Getting through Impact:

As McDonald's keeps on exploring the intricacies of an impacting world, its heritage and persevering through impact stay implanted in the texture of American culture. The Brilliant Curves, when an image of a little California café, have turned into a notorious portrayal of the American inexpensive food experience. They mean a spot to eat as well as a social standard that has molded ages of purchasers.

The tradition of McDonald's goes past the food served under those Brilliant Curves. It is an account of development, flexibility, and social effect.

McDonald's has turned into an image of American pioneering soul, a contextual in-vestigation in worldwide business achievement, and a social peculiarity that has made a permanent imprint on the cheap food industry and the more extensive social scene.

A Brilliant Heritage Moving:

The effect of McDonald's on the cheap food industry and American culture is a story that keeps on unfurling. From its progressive way to deal with inexpensive food administration to its worldwide development and impact on culinary patterns, McDonald's has been an impetus for change. The persevering through tradition of the Brilliant Curves lies in the billions of feasts filled in as well as in the social, cultural, and financial effect that traverses many years.

As McDonald's countenances the difficulties and chances representing things to come, its capacity to adjust, develop, and resound with buyers will decide the follow-ing parts of its inheritance. The Brilliant Curves, remaining as an image of the brand's persevering through impact, will keep on coaxing ages of buyers, welcoming them into an existence where cheap food, comfort, and social importance meet — a heritage moving, pushed by the persevering through soul of development and a promise to forming the way the world eats."

8.3 Reflections on Kroc's legacy and the continued growth of McDonald's

The tradition of Beam Kroc, designer of the worldwide McDonald's domain, stretches out a long ways past the domain of cheap food. An inheritance envelops business venture, development, magnanimity, and social effect. As we ponder Kroc's getting through impact and the proceeded with development of Mcdonald's, we find a story that goes past the recognizable Brilliant Curves — a story that addresses the development of business, the flexibility of a brand, and the intricacies of leaving an enduring engraving on the world.

1. **Enterprising Vision and Advancement:**
   Beam Kroc's inheritance as a business person is described by a visionary enthusiasm that rose above traditional limits. His experience with the McDonald siblings and their spearheading inexpensive food model lighted a flash of development that would rethink a whole industry. Kroc's virtuoso lay in perceiving a fruitful idea as well as in imagining its versatility on a worldwide scale.

   The innovative soul that Kroc exemplified was not simply about monetary achievement; it was tied in with reshaping the manner in which individuals experienced and devoured food. The establishment model he supported wasn't simply a business methodology; it was a plan for transforming a nearby sensation into a worldwide peculiarity. Kroc's heritage as a business visionary is a demonstration of the extraordinary force of striking thoughts and the foreknowledge to see potential open doors where others could see limits.

2. **Altruism and Social Obligation:**
   Past the meeting rooms and café kitchens, Beam Kroc's altruistic undertakings made a permanent imprint on society. The foundation of the McDonald's Establishment and the production of Ronald McDonald House Good cause (RMHC) epitomize Kroc's obligation to offering in return. These drives were not simple corporate signals; they were indications of Kroc's conviction that achievement conveyed with it an obligation to inspire networks.

   The McDonald's Establishment's emphasis on instruction and RMHC's devotion to supporting families during testing times displayed's comprehension Kroc might interpret the more extensive effect a partnership could have on society. The tradition of McDonald's isn't just about hamburgers and French fries; it's likewise about the positive impact a worldwide brand can employ to have a significant effect in the existences of people and networks.

3. **Worldwide Development and Social Reconciliation:**
   McDonald's excursion from a little San Bernardino café to a worldwide monster is a demonstration of its capacity to explore the intricacies of different societies and markets. The brand's development under Kroc's initiative was definitely not a simple replication of a format; it was a practice in social coordination. McDonald's adjusted its menu to nearby preferences, embraced provincial subtleties, and turned into an image of social trade.

   The Brilliant Curves, when an American image, changed into a widespread image that resounded across landmasses. The brand's capacity to flawlessly incorporate into different social orders addressed Kroc's comprehension that worldwide achievement required an appreciation for neighborhood inclinations.

Mcdonald's, under Kroc's stewardship, turned into a social diplomat that associated individuals through a common encounter of food and commonality.

4. **Difficulties and Flexibility:**
Kroc's inheritance isn't without any trace of difficulties; it's characterized by how he explored them. From starting battles to persuade the McDonald siblings to establishment their idea to defeating social protections and managing contentions, Kroc's process was set apart by versatility. The capacity to adjust to evolving conditions, gain from misfortunes, and advance the plan of action displayed Kroc's initiative intuition.

The difficulties McDonald's confronted, be it connected with menu extension, quality control, or general wellbeing concerns, were met with a proactive methodology. Kroc's readiness to tune in, learn, and improve turned into a sign of McDonald's capacity to get by as well as flourish in a consistently changing business scene. The tradition of flexibility and versatility stays implanted in McDonald's DNA as it keeps on advancing in light of contemporary difficulties.

5. **Influence on Work Practices:**
McDonald's impact reaches out past the bounds of the inexpensive food industry to affect work rehearses inside the more extensive help area. The diversifying model presented by Kroc sped up the brand's development as well as decentralized proprietorship. Nearby business people turned into the substance of Mcdonald's, adding to a change in the elements of work inside the business.

The accentuation on normalization, effectiveness, and preparing set industry principles for administration situated organizations. McDonald's turned into a model for functional proficiency, and its prosperity impacted rivals to embrace comparable practices. The tradition of McDonald's in molding business rehearses isn't just about making position however about setting benchmarks for preparing, client assistance, and functional greatness.

6. **Innovative Reconciliation and the Advanced Age:**
As we explore the computerized age, McDonald's keeps on being a trailblazer in coordinating innovation into its tasks. The presentation of self-administration stands, portable requesting, and conveyance administrations mirrors the brand's flexibility to changing shopper propensities. The utilization of innovation improves the client experience as well as positions McDonald's at the cutting edge of an industry going through a computerized change.

Kroc's tradition of development lives on in McDonald's obligation to keeping up to date with mechanical headways. The brand's capacity to use computerized stages for requesting, installment, and conveyance highlights its significance in reality as we know it where comfort and speed are principal. McDonald's remaining parts a contextual analysis in how a laid out brand can embrace mechanical change to meet the developing assumptions for an educated purchaser base.

7. **Marking and Social Iconography:**
The Brilliant Curves are in excess of a logo; they are social iconography that rises

above borders. How Kroc might interpret the force of marking transformed McDonald's into an image of American culture and impact. The famous plan, significant mottos, and brand characters became promoting apparatuses as well as social standards that resounded with individuals all around the world.

McDonald's isn't simply a spot to eat; a social image connotes commonality, consistency, and a common encounter. The Brilliant Curves have become inseparable from a specific approach to eating out, and their persevering through presence in the social scene is a demonstration of Kroc's understanding into the harmonious connection among brand and culture.

8. **Heritage in a Changing Culinary Scene:**

In our current reality where culinary patterns advance quickly, McDonald's heritage is reflected in its getting through works of art as well as in its capacity to adjust to evolving tastes.

The presentation of better menu choices, the accentuation on supportability, and the affirmation of different culinary inclinations address McDonald's continuous endeavors to stay significant in a unique culinary scene.

Kroc's heritage in the culinary circle isn't just about advocating cheap food; it's tied in with impacting more extensive conversations around food decisions, healthful straightforwardness, and maintainability. As shopper inclinations keep on moving, McDonald's inheritance is a story of a brand that pays attention to its crowd, gains from culinary patterns, and stays an essential piece of the contemporary food culture.

9. **Worldwide Financial Effect:**

McDonald's isn't simply an inexpensive food chain; it's a financial force to be reckoned with a worldwide impression. The brand's tasks set out business open doors, support neighborhood providers, and add to monetary biological systems all over the planet. The establishment model presented by Kroc enabled nearby business visionaries, cultivating monetary development and advancement in different networks.

The monetary effect of McDonald's stretches out past its cafés to contact different areas, from horticulture and food handling to planned operations and retail. Kroc's heritage, in this specific circumstance, is about more than making a fruitful business; it's tied in with adding to the financial dynamic quality of networks on a worldwide scale.

10. **Proceeded with Development and Future Difficulties:**

As McDonald's looks toward the future, its direction is a mix of respecting custom and embracing development. The brand's obligation to supportability, advanced mix, and menu development mirrors a comprehension of the always changing elements of purchaser assumptions. McDonald's continuous development isn't just about extending the quantity of cafés; it's tied in with remaining important in our current reality where shopper decisions and cultural assumptions keep on advancing.

The difficulties McDonald's appearances in the 21st hundred years, from addressing natural worries to fulfilling the need for better choices, are open doors for the brand to exhibit the getting through standards of versatility and obligation that are essential for Kroc's heritage. The proceeded with development of McDonald's isn't simply a demonstration of its past progress yet an impression of its capacity to explore a complicated and dynamic scene.

A Heritage Moving:

Beam Kroc's inheritance is a story that keeps on unfurling with each passing age. A heritage lives in the notable Brilliant Curves as well as in the steadily developing circular segment of McDonald's as a worldwide brand. From the beginning of a little San Bernardino eatery to the present-day presence in endless nations, McDonald's is in excess of a cheap food monster; it's a social peculiarity formed by the vision and versatility of its organizer.

As we consider Kroc's heritage and the proceeded with development of Mcdonald's, we find a story that goes past business measurements and quarterly reports. It's an account of development, flexibility, and social effect. The Brilliant Curves, remaining as a guide of commonality and association, address a brand as well as a heritage moving — an inheritance that will keep on forming the way the world eats, interfaces, and encounters the getting through effect of Mcdonald's."

Chapter 9

Challenges and Controversies

"Mcdonald's: Exploring Difficulties and Contentions in the Brilliant Excursion"

The brilliant excursion of Mcdonald's, while set apart by phenomenal achievement and worldwide impact, has not been resistant to difficulties and contentions. From general wellbeing concerns and ecological reactions to work questions and fights in court, McDonald's has endured storms that tried the flexibility of the notable Brilliant Curves. This investigation dives into the diverse difficulties and contentions that McDonald's has looked all through its development, revealing insight into the intricacies that accompany being a worldwide inexpensive food goliath.

1. **Nourishing Reactions and General Wellbeing Concerns:**
   One of the getting through debates that has shadowed McDonald's over its time is the evaluate of its menu contributions and their effect on general wellbeing. As inexpensive food became inseparable from accommodation, reasonableness, and speed, concerns arose about the dietary nature of the contributions at McDonald's and comparable foundations.
   Pundits highlighted the elevated degrees of immersed fats, sugars, and sodium in some menu things, crediting them to medical problems like stoutness, diabetes, and cardiovascular issues.
   The universal presence of McDonald's and the ubiquity of its items made it a point of convergence in more extensive conversations about the job of cheap food in general wellbeing. The organization confronted examination and legitimate difficulties, for certain claims endeavoring to consider McDonald's responsible for wellbeing related issues.
   In light of these worries, McDonald's executed different changes to its menu, presenting better choices, giving wholesome data, and advancing adjusted eating.

The discussions encompassing wholesome reactions highlighted the more extensive cultural discussions about diet, way of life, and corporate obligation.

2. **Work Practices and Specialist's Freedoms:**

As quite possibly of the biggest boss on the planet, McDonald's has been a point of convergence for conversations on work practices and laborers' freedoms. The organization's diversifying model, which engages nearby business people to possess and work McDonald's eateries, carried with it intricacies connected with work connections, wages, and working circumstances.

Work questions and strikes, both in the US and globally, have been essential for McDonald's account. Laborers and work activists have upheld for higher wages, worked on working circumstances, and the option to unionize. The organization's reactions to these difficulties, including wage increments and changes in benefits, have mirrored a continuous exchange about the harmony among productivity and the prosperity of its labor force.

McDonald's process through work related contentions mirrors the more extensive cultural talk about pay imbalance, laborers' privileges, and the obligations of enormous organizations. The organization's position and activities in addressing these worries add to forming the continuous story around fair work rehearses in the cheap food industry.

3. **Natural Reactions and Supportability Difficulties:**

The broad worldwide impression of McDonald's has brought it under a microscope for its natural effect. Concerns have been raised about issues going from deforestation connected to obtaining meat to the natural outcomes of bundling waste related with its items. The utilization of single-use plastics, specifically, has been a disputed matter.

Natural activists and buyers the same have called for more noteworthy supportability rehearses inside the cheap food industry, encouraging organizations like McDonald's to take on eco-accommodating measures and diminish their carbon impression. The test for McDonald's has been to adjust the requests of large scale manufacturing and worldwide appropriation with the developing basic for earth capable practices.

In light of these reactions, McDonald's has dedicated to supportability objectives, including endeavors to source hamburger capably, lessen bundling waste, and upgrade energy productivity in its activities. These drives mirror the more extensive change in shopper assumptions and cultural requests for organizations to participate in feasible practices effectively.

4. **Social Awareness and Nearby Variation:**

The worldwide extension of McDonald's has not been without social difficulties. As the brand wandered into different nations and districts, it confronted the errand of adjusting its contributions to nearby preferences and inclinations. The thought of social awareness became necessary to McDonald's capacity to incorporate into various social orders without undermining its center personality effectively.

Contentions have arisen when McDonald's confronted opposition or reaction from nearby networks and social idealists who saw the brand as an image of Westernization. Adjusting the worldwide McDonald's image with the requirement for nearby transformation turned into a sensitive dance, and occasions of social conflicts provoked the organization to reconsider its procedures in specific business sectors.

McDonald's reaction to these provokes has involved a pledge to glocalization — fitting menus, showcasing, and even café plans to line up with neighborhood societies while keeping a durable worldwide brand personality. The expectation to learn and adapt in exploring social responsive qualities stays a continuous part of McDonald's worldwide excursion.

5. **Fights in court and Corporate Obligation:**

   Mcdonald's, as a worldwide organization, has ended up entrapped in fights in court that cross a range of issues. From high-profile claims connected with wellbeing concerns, for example, the scandalous "McLibel" case in the Unified Realm, to legitimate difficulties around work practices and protected innovation, the organization has been a continuous prosecutor.

   Lawful contentions have tried the flexibility of McDonald's as well as incited the organization to reevaluate its practices and arrangements. Whether confronting claims of misdirecting promoting, wage infringement, or establishment debates, McDonald's reactions have molded the two its corporate picture and the lawful scene for global enterprises.

   The organization's obligation to corporate obligation is clear in its reactions to lawful difficulties. Drives to address concerns, carry out changes in strategic approaches, and draw in with partners mirror a comprehension of the developing assumptions put on huge companies in the 21st 100 years.

6. **Promoting and Publicizing Examination:**

   McDonald's has been at the bleeding edge of the inexpensive food industry's promoting and publicizing scene, making notorious missions and critical characters. Notwithstanding, the brand has additionally confronted investigation for its showcasing rehearses, particularly concerning the focusing of kids and the advancement of less nutritious menu things.

   Pundits contend that forceful promoting to youngsters adds to unfortunate dietary patterns and can have long haul ramifications for general wellbeing. Legitimate activities and calls for stricter guidelines on cheap food publicizing, particularly when coordinated at a more youthful crowd, have provoked McDonald's and other industry players to reexamine their showcasing procedures.

   Accordingly, McDonald's has acquainted changes with its publicizing works on, including advancing better menu choices, giving wholesome data, and partaking in broad drives to address showcasing related concerns. The discussions encompassing showcasing rehearses feature the continuous discussion about the moral elements of publicizing, particularly in businesses with potential well-being suggestions.

7. **Advancing Shopper Inclinations and Industry Disturbance:**
The inexpensive food industry, including Mcdonald's, has encountered critical disturbance driven by changing purchaser inclinations. The ascent of quick easygoing eating, interest for better choices, and the accentuation on new, privately obtained fixings have introduced difficulties for conventional inexpensive food chains.

Mcdonald's, with its laid out brand and normalized menu, has needed to explore the developing scene of shopper tastes and assumptions. The difficulties have provoked the organization to present menu advancements, including better decisions, and to adjust its tasks to line up with contemporary culinary patterns.

The disturbances in the business highlight the requirement for McDonald's to stay deft and receptive to moving shopper inclinations. The continuous test lies in finding some kind of harmony between keeping up with the commonality that characterizes the McDonald's insight and taking care of the different and advancing requests of current shoppers.

8. **Public Discernment and Brand Picture:**

The public impression of McDonald's has been formed by its prosperity as well as by the discussions and difficulties it has confronted. The brand's picture has been a subject of public talk, with discusses going from its effect on wellbeing to its part in social globalization. These discernments, whether positive or negative, have impacted customer mentalities and ways of behaving.

Overseeing public discernment requires an essential methodology, and McDonald's has put resources into drives to improve its image picture. This incorporates straightforward correspondence about obtaining rehearses, dietary data, and maintainability endeavors. Be that as it may, the test stays dynamic, as the brand should explore the always changing scene of popular assessment and cultural assumptions.

The debates and difficulties looked by McDonald's have been necessary to its development, provoking transformations, developments, and an uplifted familiarity with its job in the public eye. As the brand keeps on wrestling with these intricacies, it is a demonstration of the continuous discourse between a worldwide corporate substance and the different networks it serves.

Exploring the Brilliant Archipelago of Difficulties:
The brilliant archipelago of Mcdonald's, traversing mainlands and societies, has endured tempests of difficulties and debates. From the dietary focus on its menu to the complexities of worldwide social incorporation, McDonald's has shown a strength that reaches out past the business domain. The organization's capacity to explore and answer moves reflects not exclusively its obligation to benefit yet in addition acknowledgment of the more extensive obligations accompany worldwide impact.

As McDonald's proceeds with its excursion into the future, the difficulties and debates will endure, molded by cultural movements, innovative headways, and the consistently advancing assumptions for shoppers. The Brilliant Curves, remaining as an image of commonality and association, address a cheap food goliath as well as a worldwide substance exploring the intricacies of contemporary presence — an excursion that unfurls in the public eye, with each challenge met and discussion tended to forming the continuous story of McDonald's in the cutting edge world."

9.1 Examination of controversies and criticisms faced by McDonald's

"Past the Brilliant Curves: An Inside and out Assessment of Discussions and Reactions Looked by Mcdonald's"

The excursion of Mcdonald's, set apart by famous Brilliant Curves and a worldwide presence, has not been without any trace of debates and reactions. As the inexpensive food monster extended its scope and turned into a vital piece of current culture, it ended up under the investigation of different partners — from wellbeing backers and earthy people to work activists and customers. This investigation dives into the diverse debates and reactions that have formed McDonald's story, revealing insight into the difficulties inborn in being a worldwide social peculiarity.

1. **Healthful Discussions and the Inexpensive Food Discussion:**
   At the front of McDonald's discussions is the continuous discussion encompassing the healthful substance of its menu contributions. As the cheap food industry blossomed in the last 50% of the twentieth hundred years, McDonald's turned into an image of helpful, reasonable, and quick dinners. Nonetheless, the prominence of its menu things, especially burgers, fries, and sweet refreshments, drew analysis for their commitment to medical problems like weight, diabetes, and coronary illness.

   Pundits contend that the elevated degrees of salt, immersed fats, and sugars in McDonald's items are adverse to general wellbeing. The scandalous narrative "Super Size Me" further intensified concerns, displaying the potential wellbeing chances related with an eating regimen intensely dependent on inexpensive food. McDonald's has confronted claims, including the broadly broadcasted "McLibel" case, where it was blamed for deceiving publicizing and adding to count calories related medical issues.

   In light of these reactions, McDonald's has presented better menu choices, including plates of mixed greens, barbecued chicken, and organic product. The organization has additionally put forth attempts to give healthful data, both in cafés and on the web, to enable purchasers to settle on informed decisions. In any case, the wholesome discussions keep on highlighting more extensive cultural discussions about the job of cheap food in general wellbeing.

2. **Work Practices and the Battle for Laborers' Freedoms:**
   As one of the biggest businesses universally, McDonald's has been a point of convergence in conversations about work practices and laborers' privileges. The

diversifying model, which permits nearby business people to work McDonald's cafés, presented intricacies with regards to representative relations, wages, and working circumstances.

Work strikes and fights, frequently drove by cheap food laborers pushing for higher wages and worked on working circumstances, definitely stand out around the world. The "Battle for $15" development in the US, requiring a lowest pay permitted by law of $15 each hour, built up some decent momentum with McDonald's laborers taking part in the exhibits. The organization confronted reactions for its apparent protection from wage increments and claims of work infringement.

Accordingly, McDonald's has carried out changes, including wage increments for laborers at organization possessed cafés and support for franchisees who decide to raise compensation. The organization's obligation to corporate obligation and its reaction to work related contentions mirror a continuous discourse about fair pay and the privileges of laborers in the cheap food industry.

3. **Natural Worries and Supportability Difficulties:**
The worldwide size of McDonald's tasks has set it under the natural spotlight, with worries going from deforestation connected to meat obtaining to the biological effect of bundling waste. Natural activists and customers have called for expanded supportability measures, encouraging McDonald's to embrace eco-accommodating practices and lessen its carbon impression.

The utilization of single-use plastics, a critical supporter of ecological corruption, has been an industrious issue. Mcdonald's, with its immense number of everyday exchanges, faces the test of adjusting the accommodation of dispensable bundling with the basic to lessen natural mischief.

Accordingly, McDonald's has dedicated to supportability objectives, including endeavors to source maintainable meat, diminish bundling waste, and improve energy effectiveness in its activities. The organization's excursion towards more noteworthy maintainability mirrors the more extensive change in buyer assumptions and cultural requests for mindful corporate practices.

4. **Social Responsiveness and Worldwide Variation:**
As McDonald's ventured into different social scenes, it experienced difficulties connected with social responsiveness and neighborhood transformation. The brand, frequently seen as an image of Americanization, confronted obstruction in certain districts where it was seen as a danger to nearby culinary practices and social personality.

Contentions emitted when McDonald's experienced reaction from networks that opposed its presence. Cases of social conflicts provoked the organization to reexamine its procedures and move toward in specific business sectors. The test lies in finding some kind of harmony between keeping a strong worldwide brand personality and regarding nearby preferences and customs.

McDonald's reaction has been to embrace glocalization — adjusting menus, advertising, and even café plans to line up with neighborhood societies. The expectation to learn and adapt in exploring social awarenesses stays a continuous part of McDonald's worldwide excursion, requiring constant transformation and commitment with assorted networks.

5. **Fights in court and the Intricacy of Corporate Obligation:**
   Mcdonald's, as a worldwide company, has been ensnared in fights in court that range a range of issues. High-profile claims, for example, the "McLibel" case in the Unified Realm, highlighted the difficulties looked by the organization in exploring the legitimate scene. Charges of misdirecting promoting, worries about wellbeing effects, and debates with franchisees have added to a perplexing snare of lawful difficulties.

   The legitimate debates have incited McDonald's to reevaluate its practices and arrangements. The organization's reactions to lawful moves reflect not exclusively its obligation to corporate obligation yet additionally how its might interpret the advancing assumptions put on enormous partnerships in the 21st 100 years. McDonald's has executed changes in light of lawful activities, displaying an eagerness to adjust to cultural movements and moral contemplations.

6. **Promoting and Publicizing Examination:**
   Mcdonald's, eminent for its creative promoting and notable publicizing efforts, has additionally confronted examination for its showcasing rehearses. One critical area of concern spins around the advertising of less nutritious menu things, particularly when designated at youngsters. Pundits contend that forceful promoting adds to unfortunate dietary patterns, especially among more youthful buyers.

   Legitimate activities and calls for stricter guidelines on cheap food promoting, especially those focused on youngsters, have provoked McDonald's and other industry players to reconsider their showcasing methodologies. The discussions feature the moral components of publicizing in enterprises with potential wellbeing suggestions.

   Accordingly, McDonald's has acquainted changes with its publicizing works on, accentuating the advancement of better menu choices, giving nourishing data, and taking part in broad drives to address promoting related concerns. The continuous discourse about dependable promoting rehearses mirrors the developing cultural assumptions about straightforwardness and responsibility.

7. **Advancing Buyer Inclinations and Industry Disturbance:**
   The inexpensive food industry, including Mcdonald's, has confronted interruption energized by changing customer inclinations. The ascent of quick easygoing eating, an interest for better choices, and an emphasis on new, privately obtained fixings have introduced difficulties for conventional inexpensive food chains.

   Mcdonald's, with its normalized menu and laid out brand, has needed to explore the developing scene of purchaser tastes. The difficulties have provoked the organization to present menu advancements, including better decisions, and to adjust its tasks to line up with contemporary culinary patterns.

The disturbances in the business highlight the requirement for McDonald's to stay deft and receptive to moving shopper inclinations. The continuous test lies in finding some kind of harmony between keeping up with the commonality that characterizes the McDonald's insight and taking special care of the different and advancing requests of present day shoppers.

8. **Public Discernment and Brand Picture:**

The public impression of McDonald's has been molded by its victories as well as by the discussions and difficulties it has confronted. The brand's picture has been a subject of public talk, with discusses going from its effect on wellbeing to its job in social globalization. These discernments, whether positive or negative, have affected purchaser perspectives and ways of behaving.

Overseeing public discernment requires an essential methodology, and McDonald's has put resources into drives to improve its image picture. Straightforward correspondence about obtaining rehearses, nourishing data, and manageability endeavors are important for the organization's endeavors to introduce a more capable and buyer cognizant picture. Nonetheless, the test stays dynamic, as the brand should explore the consistently changing scene of general assessment and cultural assumptions.

Exploring the Intricate Territory of Reactions:

Mcdonald's, as a symbolic figure in the worldwide cheap food scene, explores a perplexing territory of reactions and discussions. From nourishing worries and work practices to natural effect and social transformation, the difficulties looked by McDonald's are all around as different as its menu contributions. The organization's reactions to these difficulties mirror a comprehension of the advancing assumptions put on partnerships in the 21st 100 years.

As McDonald's keeps on navigating the complexities of the cheap food industry, the assessment of discussions and reactions becomes essential to its continuous account. The Brilliant Curves, standing as images of comfort and commonality as well as reference points of liability, address a worldwide element that wrestles with the intricacies of contemporary presence. In tending to reactions, McDonald's shapes not exclusively its own direction yet additionally adds to more extensive discussions about corporate obligation, cultural assumptions, and the always advancing elements of the cheap food industry."

9.2 Challenges in the changing landscape of the fast-food industry

"Adjusting to the Range of Progress: Difficulties in the Advancing Scene of the Cheap Food Industry"

The cheap food industry, a dynamic and consistently evolving scene, has been a pot of difficulties and variations for key part like Mcdonald's. As customer inclinations shift, cultural assumptions develop, and mechanical headways rethink the feasting experience, cheap food chains face a horde of snags in keeping up with significance, maintainability, and buyer trust. This investigation digs into the multi-layered difficulties that McDonald's and its peers experience in the advancing cheap food biological system.

1. **Culinary Advancement and Wellbeing Awareness:**
   One of the essential difficulties in the cheap food industry rotates around the advancing assumptions for purchasers in regards to culinary decisions and wellbeing cognizance. As society turns out to be progressively wellbeing centered, there is a developing interest for better menu choices that line up with different dietary inclinations, including veggie lover, vegetarian, and sans gluten decisions. Customary cheap food menus, frequently connected with liberal and calorie-thick contributions, face examination as shoppers look for straightforwardness in dietary data. Mcdonald's, as a cheap food monster, wrestles with the fragile equilibrium of holding mark things while presenting better other options. The test lies in satisfying the needs of wellbeing cognizant purchasers without estranging those looking for the recognizable solace of exemplary cheap food charge.

   Accordingly, McDonald's has presented plates of mixed greens, barbecued choices, and different other options, intending to take care of a more wellbeing cognizant customers. The culinary development inside the cheap food industry mirrors a more extensive cultural shift towards careful eating and represents a ceaseless test for brands to remain receptive to changing preferences while safeguarding their center character.

2. **Innovative Mix and Computerized Change:**
   The coming of innovation has introduced another period of accommodation and customization in the cheap food industry. Portable requesting, self-administration stands, and conveyance applications have become indispensable parts of the feasting experience. In any case, the quick speed of mechanical development presents the two open doors and difficulties for cheap food chains.

   Mcdonald's, in its quest for mechanical mix, faces the test of taking on new frameworks as well as guaranteeing a consistent and easy to understand insight for clients. The shift towards advanced stages requires interest in foundation, representative preparation, and network safety measures to defend delicate information.

   The continuous test lies in tackling innovation to upgrade the client experience without compromising the human touch that characterizes customary eating. McDonald's and other inexpensive food chains wrestle with finding some kind of harmony among productivity and the individual touch that has been a sign of the business.

3. **Supportability and Moral Obtaining:**
   As ecological cognizance turns into a significant thought for buyers, the cheap food industry faces expanding strain to take on maintainable practices and moral

obtaining. Issues, for example, single-use plastics, deforestation connected to hamburger creation, and waste administration are at the front of manageability challenges.

Mcdonald's, with its immense worldwide impression, experiences the test of adjusting its store network with reasonable and moral practices. Adjusting the requests of large scale manufacturing with earth capable decisions requires key independent direction and cooperation with providers. Furthermore, conveying these drives to shoppers is vital for building trust and believability.

Accordingly, McDonald's has dedicated to manageability objectives, including capable obtaining of meat and decreasing bundling waste. The test endures as the business explores the intricacies of executing and conveying maintainability rehearses while keeping up with cost-viability.

4. **Moving Buyer Assumptions and Culinary Variety:**
The cutting edge buyer is described by a different sense of taste and a craving for culinary investigation. Cheap food chains face the test of adjusting to the moving assumptions for shoppers who look for comfort as well as a different scope of flavors and social impacts.

Mcdonald's, generally connected with normalized menus, fights with the test of giving a changed culinary encounter while keeping up with functional effectiveness. The ascent of quick relaxed eating and the ubiquity of worldwide cooking styles add layers of intricacy to the cheap food scene, requiring readiness in menu advancement and advertising techniques.

Accordingly, McDonald's and comparative chains have presented restricted time contributions, territorial fortes, and coordinated efforts with prestigious gourmet experts to take care of different preferences. The test lies in remaining sensitive to culinary patterns, answering local inclinations, and making a menu that requests to an expansive range of purchasers.

5. **Administrative Consistence and Wellbeing Guidelines:**
The inexpensive food industry works inside an administrative system that oversees wellbeing and security principles. Fulfilling these guidelines, especially in regions like food planning, stockpiling, and representative cleanliness, is a non-stop test for cheap food chains.

Mcdonald's, with its broad worldwide presence, faces the intricacy of sticking to different administrative conditions. Neighborhood guidelines, wellbeing codes, and sanitation principles shift, requiring careful thoughtfulness regarding consistence. The test reaches out to overseeing supply chains to guarantee the quality and security of fixings.

Accordingly, McDonald's puts resources into thorough preparation programs, quality control measures, and joint efforts with providers to maintain wellbeing guidelines. The test perseveres as the business wrestles with an advancing administrative scene and increased public investigation of wellbeing and security rehearses.

6. **Monetary Variances and Valuing Methodologies:**

The cheap food industry isn't invulnerable to monetary vacillations, and chains like McDonald's explore the test of adjusting to changing financial circumstances. Monetary slumps can affect customer ways of managing money, impacting decisions in feasting out and food utilization.

Keeping up with reasonableness while offering quality food turns into a fragile difficult exercise. Mcdonald's, as a worldwide brand, faces the test of formulating evaluating systems that take special care of different financial settings without settling on apparent worth and quality.

Accordingly, McDonald's has presented esteem menus, special estimating, and packaging choices to interest thrifty customers. The test lies in persistently reevaluating evaluating systems to stay cutthroat and open in the midst of monetary vulnerabilities.

7. **Ability Procurement and Labor force Difficulties:**

The inexpensive food industry depends vigorously on a different and frequently transient labor force. Selecting and holding ability in a serious work market present difficulties for chains like Mcdonald's. Issues, for example, wage assumptions, representative advantages, and potential open doors for profession development are basic contemplations in ability procurement.

McDonald's appearances the test of drawing in talented and roused representatives while addressing concerns connected with wages and working circumstances. The transient idea of a cheap food occupations adds intricacy to labor force the executives, requiring interests in preparing and improvement programs.

Accordingly, McDonald's has executed drives, for example, schooling help projects and profession improvement amazing open doors. The test endures as the business explores the more extensive talk around fair wages, work privileges, and representative prosperity.

8. **Pandemic Versatility and Flexibility:**

The Coronavirus pandemic has acquainted phenomenal difficulties with the inexpensive food industry, requiring flexibility and versatility. Lockdowns, limitations on eat in administrations, and changes in purchaser conduct have constrained anchors like McDonald's to reevaluate functional models and embrace better approaches for serving clients.

McDonald's appearances the test of guaranteeing the security of the two clients and representatives while exploring the monetary vulnerabilities achieved by the pandemic. The fast reception of contactless requesting, conveyance administrations, and drive-through choices represents the business' reaction to the developing scene.

Accordingly, McDonald's has carried out security conventions, extended conveyance choices, and put resources into innovation to improve contactless encounters.

The test lies in supporting these variations and staying coordinated as the business proceeds to recuperate and rethink its post-pandemic personality.

Exploring the Transition of Progress in Cheap Food:

The cheap food industry, a ceaselessly moving landscape, presents a range of difficulties that request consistent variation and development. For Mcdonald's, the famous Brilliant Curves become an image of comfort as well as a demonstration of the brand's capacity to explore the transition of progress.

As culinary inclinations develop, innovation reshapes the feasting experience, and maintainability becomes central, McDonald's and its counterparts wind up at the bleeding edge of an industry in never-ending movement. The difficulties looked in giving assorted culinary encounters, embracing mechanical progressions, and satisfying administrative guidelines are obstacles as well as any open doors for development and flexibility.

The Brilliant Curves, remaining as sentinels in the cheap food scene, represent a brand as well as an excursion — an excursion of exploring difficulties, adjusting to change, and proceeding to act as a worldwide symbol of the inexpensive food experience."

9.3 McDonald's response and adaptations in the face of criticism

"Brilliant Variations: McDonald's Reaction to Reactions and Forming What's to come"

As one of the most unmistakable brands internationally, McDonald's has been no more bizarre to analysis and examination. Whether confronting difficulties connected with sustenance, work rehearses, ecological effect, or social responsiveness, McDonald's reaction to reactions has been essential in forming its direction. This investigation digs into the diverse manners by which McDonald's has adjusted and answered analysis, displaying the brand's strength and obligation to advancing with the times.

1. **Dietary Reactions:**

   Confronting persevering reactions in regards to the dietary substance of its menu, McDonald's has found a way essential ways to address worries about the effect of its contributions on general wellbeing. Perceiving the developing pattern of wellbeing cognizant customers, the organization has rolled out significant improvements to its menu.

   McDonald's presented better other options, like plates of mixed greens, barbecued chicken choices, and natural product, to give a more adjusted determination to clients. The expansion of dietary data on menus and bundling further enables purchasers to go with informed decisions. This straightforwardness mirrors McDonald's obligation to tending to wholesome reactions by offering a range of choices that take care of shifting dietary inclinations.

   Also, the organization has taken part in reformulation endeavors to lessen salt, sugar, and immersed fats in specific menu things. By answering proactively to wholesome reactions, McDonald's adjusts to changing shopper assumptions as well as positions itself as a brand worried about the prosperity of its benefactors.

2. **Work Practices and Laborers' Privileges:**
The inexpensive food industry, including Mcdonald's, has confronted investigation in regards to work practices and laborers' privileges. Reactions connected with low wages and inadequate advantages incited McDonald's to rethink its way to deal with its labor force. Because of the "Battle for $15" development and other work driven drives, the organization carried out changes to address a portion of these worries.

McDonald's focused on expanding compensation for workers at organization possessed eateries, flagging an acknowledgment of the significance of fair remuneration. Additionally, the organization has upheld franchisees in their endeavors to give serious wages and advantages. By effectively captivating with the talk around laborers' freedoms, McDonald's adjusts its work practices to line up with developing cultural assumptions.

The execution of instructive help projects and amazing open doors for professional success additionally mirrors McDonald's obligation to sustaining its labor force. These transformations address reactions as well as position McDonald's as a business receptive to the changing elements of the work scene.

3. **Natural Maintainability:**
In the midst of developing worries about natural maintainability, McDonald's has confronted reactions connected with its biological impression, especially in regions like bundling and obtaining. Accordingly, the organization has committed to maintainability, recognizing its job in tending to natural difficulties.

McDonald's laid out aggressive objectives, including a guarantee to source all visitor bundling from sustainable, reused, or confirmed sources by 2025. The organization has likewise promised to make huge decreases in ozone harming substance discharges and further develop water effectiveness in its production network. These responsibilities highlight McDonald's endeavors to adjust to a changing natural scene and contribute emphatically to the planet.

In addition, McDonald's has effectively participated in drives to diminish single-use plastics, investigating elective bundling arrangements. The organization's obligation to maintainable obtaining of hamburger and mindful horticultural practices mirrors an all encompassing way to deal with tending to natural reactions. McDonald's isn't just answering current natural worries but on the other hand is situating itself as a forerunner in maintainable practices inside the cheap food industry.

4. **Social Awareness and Neighborhood Transformation:**
The worldwide extension of McDonald's has carried social aversion to the front of its difficulties. Reactions about the brand being an image of Westernization provoked McDonald's to reconsider its way to deal with social variation. Instead of forcing a uniform worldwide personality, McDonald's has embraced the

idea of glocalization — adjusting its contributions to neighborhood tastes and inclinations while keeping a durable worldwide brand.

The organization's menu reflects territorial strengths and socially impacted things, displaying a guarantee to regarding nearby culinary customs. This approach tends to reactions of social lack of care as well as cultivates a feeling of inclusivity in the different business sectors where McDonald's works.

Past menu variation, McDonald's has custom fitted its showcasing techniques to resound with nearby societies. Joint efforts with neighborhood powerhouses, celebrations, and local area drives represent the brand's commitment to being a positive and socially mindful presence in different districts. By effectively answering reactions connected with social responsiveness, McDonald's explores the complexities of worldwide extension with versatility and regard.

5. **Promoting and Publicizing Practices:**

Mcdonald's, a trailblazer in the cheap food industry's promoting scene, has confronted examination for its publicizing rehearses, particularly those focusing on youngsters. Pundits contend that forceful advertising adds to unfortunate dietary patterns and postures long haul wellbeing gambles.

Accordingly, McDonald's has rolled out huge improvements to its advertising procedures. The organization focused on advancing better menu choices in its promoting, accentuating straightforwardness about nourishing data, and partaking in far reaching drives to address worries about publicizing to youngsters.

In addition, McDonald's has changed its Cheerful Feast contributions to incorporate better choices and cutoff calorie content. These variations answer reactions as well as position McDonald's as a brand that focuses on the prosperity of its most youthful customers. By adjusting its promoting practices to wellbeing cognizant patterns, McDonald's grandstands its obligation to capable publicizing.

6. **Innovative Coordination and Advanced Change:**

The cheap food industry's hug of innovation has incited McDonald's to adjust its activities to the computerized age. Confronting reactions connected with request precision, stand by times, and the general eating experience, McDonald's has put vigorously in mechanical combination to improve client comfort.

The presentation of self-administration booths, versatile requesting, and conveyance administrations addresses McDonald's reaction to the changing elements of purchaser inclinations. These mechanical transformations address reactions as well as position McDonald's at the cutting edge of development inside the business.

Moreover, McDonald's has embraced information investigation to customize the client experience, offering designated advancements and dependability programs. By utilizing innovation, McDonald's tends to reactions connected with functional productivity as well as improves its seriousness in the advanced period.

7. **Pandemic Flexibility and Versatility:**

The extraordinary difficulties presented by the Coronavirus pandemic constrained McDonald's to adjust quickly to evolving conditions. The conclusion of eat in administrations, limitations on in-person feasting, and changes in purchaser conduct required fast acclimations to the organization's functional model.

McDonald's answered by extending its conveyance choices, presenting contactless requesting and installment, and focusing on drive-through administrations. These variations not just tended to the prompt difficulties presented by the pandemic yet in addition situated McDonald's as a brand fit for strength and flexibility even with unexpected conditions.

Additionally, the pandemic highlighted the significance of wellbeing and security measures. McDonald's carried out thorough security conventions, including upgraded cleaning systems and contactless encounters, showing a guarantee to the prosperity of the two clients and representatives. By answering really to the difficulties of the pandemic, McDonald's exhibited its capacity to adjust and flourish in a quickly evolving scene.

8. **Local area Commitment and Social Obligation:**

As a worldwide brand, McDonald's has perceived the significance of local area commitment and social obligation. Reactions connected with the apparent effect of cheap food chains on nearby networks provoked McDonald's to proactively participate in drives that contribute emphatically to society.

The organization has been engaged with altruistic endeavors, supporting foundations, and local area improvement projects. Schooling help programs for representatives, particularly as far as schooling cost help, embody McDonald's obligation to social obligation. By effectively taking part in local area building drives, McDonald's tends to reactions connected with its cultural effect and positions itself as a dependable corporate resident.

Forming Tomorrow through Versatile Reactions:

McDonald's excursion, interspersed by reactions and difficulties, is a demonstration of its capacity to adjust and answer really. By addressing concerns connected with nourishment, work rehearses, manageability, social awareness, and that's just the beginning, McDonald's has explored analysis as well as molded its future direction.

The Brilliant Curves, representative of McDonald's worldwide personality, stand as a brand as well as a unique substance fit for development. Through essential variations, proactive reactions, and a guarantee to cultural assumptions, McDonald's keeps on assuming a crucial part in the cheap food scene. As it faces new difficulties not too far off, McDonald's versatile reactions will keep on characterizing its heritage in the steadily impacting universe of cheap food."

www.ingramcontent.com/pod-product-compliance
Lightning Source LLC
LaVergne TN
LVHW011409040325
804969LV00011B/579